THE BLACK BADGE

Deputy United States Marshal
Bass Reeves
from Slave to Heroic Lawman

Paul L. Brady

THE BLACK BADGE

Deputy United States Marshal
Bass Reeves
from Slave to Heroic Lawman

Paul L. Brady

Milligan Books  California

Copyright © 2005 by Paul L. Brady
Atlanta, Georgia
All rights reserved
Printed and bound in the United States of America

Distributed by:
Milligan Books, Inc.
1425 W. Manchester Blvd., Suite C
Los Angeles, California 90047
(323) 750-3592
(323) 750-2886 Fax

Formatting/Cover Design by Chris Ebuehi/Graphic Options
Los Angeles, CA

First Printing April 2005
10 9 8 7 6 5 4 3 2 1

ISBN # 0-9759654-5-X

No part of this book may be reproduced in whole or in part, in any form or by any means, electronic or mechanical, including photocopying, recording or by any information storage and retrieval system, without permission in writing from the author. Direct all inquiries to Milligan Books, Inc.

CONTENTS

PREFACE VII

PROLOGUE
The Prophecy XI

CHAPTER ONE
Born in Bondage 1

CHAPTER TWO
Path to Freedom 11

CHAPTER THREE
Freedom 19

CHAPTER FOUR
Mixed Blessings 33

CHAPTER FIVE
The Best Laid Plans 47

CHAPTER SIX
Deputy Marshal Bass Reeves 55

CHAPTER SEVEN
Enforcing the Law 67

CHAPTER EIGHT
The Ties That Bind 77

CHAPTER NINE
Rumors, Repudiation and Reputation 93

CHAPTER TEN
The Trial 109

CHAPTER ELEVEN
Go West Young (White) Man 123

CHAPTER TWELVE
The Law and the Lawless 137

CHAPTER THIRTEEN
Father and Son 159

CHAPTER FOURTEEN
Devotion to Duty 167

CHAPTER FIFTEEN
Above The Law 175

CHAPTER SIXTEEN
Betrayal and Burial of Bass Reeves 193

CHAPTER SEVENTEEN
Newspaper Articles 203

PICTORIAL PORTFOLIO 213

SELECTED BIBLIOGRAPHY 229

REFERENCES 235

PREFACE

Perhaps no era symbolizes America's history more than the nation's western movement. The role of the frontier lawman during this period is legendary; the Texas Rangers, Wild Bill Hickok, Wyatt Earp, Bat Masterson, and other highly publicized lawmen are acclaimed as dauntless heroes.

While many exploits of western peace officers sprang from half-truths, myths, and fertile imagination, the worthy accomplishments of Deputy United States Marshal Bass Reeves have been overlooked by historians and western writers. As noted in the following 1901 publication:

> *Among the numerous deputy marshals that have ridden for the Paris (Texas), Fort Smith, (Arkansas) and Indian Territory courts, none have met with more hairbreadth escapes or have effected more hazardous arrests than Bass Reeves of Muskogee...[who] fears nothing that moves and breathes ... Several bad men have gone to their long home for refusing to halt when commanded to by Bass.*[1]

Appointed in 1875 by Hanging Judge Isaac C. Parker, Bass Reeves' career spanned over 30 years under seven marshals in the crime-ridden Indian Territory, (the area later to become Oklahoma). Bass also became the first Black man to serve as a

Federal officer on the western frontier. For his outstanding contribution to frontier justice, Bass Reeves, my great-uncle, was inducted in 1992 into the Hall of Great Westerners of the National Cowboy Hall of Fame in Oklahoma City. Accepting the honor on behalf of my uncle, I could not help recall a similar occasion 20 years earlier when I was appointed a Federal judge. I thought of Uncle Bass on that occasion too, not merely because we are members of the same family, but because both of us were dedicated to serving the rule of law. We were both honored by these appointments, but the conditions of his life filled those moments. Uncle Bass, ironically, had been born a slave, and now I was placed in a position to determine the rights of persons under the same Constitution that allowed him to be determined chattel property with no rights whatsoever. This is the story of his rise from the lowest status in society to eminence as a Federal law enforcement officer.

This biography has been more than 60 years in the making. It is a story not only of one extraordinary man, all but overlooked in the history books; it is also a story of my family, and Great Uncle Bass in particular. The people in this accounting are my dad, aunts, grandmother and cousins. The compilation of the life of Bass Reeves is not merely the product of my modest efforts. it is instead a collective endeavor primarily involving members of my family. Throughout the 60 years, they schooled me on the exploits of this outstanding man. My close relatives served as the American version of the African 'griots,' guardians of our tribe's oral history. However, since the memorized spoken word is clearly not as durable as the written word, the Bass Reeves story cried out for documentation. Gradually, it unfolded in priceless dribs and drabs. At an early age, I began my life-long fascination with our family's legend, Bass Reeves.

Although my father, William 'Luck' Brady, died when I was only 10 years old, I still remember his accounts of adventures he shared with his Uncle Bass. In similar conversations between

1954-1966, Alice Spahn, Uncle Bass' daughter and my cousin, regaled me with accounts of his escapades. I paid rapt attention whenever any one of my elders began to reminisce about Bass Reeves. Aunt Nettie Robins, my father's older sister would visit us from Van Buren, Arkansas; each visit brought with it a Bass Reeves story. She would regale us with especially interesting and intriguing yarns about the first lawman in our family. Aunt Nettie's daughters, Ethel Burks and Ruth Robinson, recounted many additional Bass anecdotes and reconstructed treasured moments they shared during the years they lived with Granny Paralee and Grandma Janie (Bass' mother and sister respectively).

Aunt Kate Franklin, my father's younger sister, also lived in Van Buren before her death in 1961. She and her husband, Ira, recalled stories about the relationship between Bass and the Native American desperado, Cherokee Bill. Also, Aunt Kate's daughter, Mildred Landfair, the last family survivor, facilitated my research greatly for over 40 years.

Non-family members also helped me piece together the sometimes-disjointed Bass Reeves story. I am indebted to Pliney Twine, a retired attorney in Muskogee, Oklahoma, who, as a boy, knew my great uncle personally and remembered how much the community respected him. Twine's father published the Muskogee Cimeter, a Black newspaper printed before statehood.

I received numerous Bass Reeves stories from Jess Bradley, a local Muskogee historian who was quite knowledgeable about the law, lawmakers and the community. Similarly, Jim Simmons, a retired Muskogee deputy sheriff, personally knew my uncle. Zethel Chamberlain of Oklahoma City gave me research assistance in the Oklahoma, Texas and Arkansas archives.

I am also indebted to Bob Hoff, a ranger, and Juliet Galonska, Park Historian at the Fort Smith National Historic site, and Meg Hacher of the National Archives in Fort Worth, Texas. James Brewster of Los Angeles, a former Muskogee native, helped me locate and identify persons who had detailed knowledge of Bass Reeves as a lawman and a Muskogee citizen. Also, I thank Zethel Chamberlain of Oklahoma City who assisted with the research. Finally, I am very grateful to Rita Johnston, my typist.

It is with the help and blessing of all of these kind souls that I bring you the true story of Bass Reeve, slave, freeman, and Deputy U.S. Marshal.

Paul L. Brady
Atlanta, April 2005

PROLOGUE
The Prophecy

Murder was a hanging offense in Judge Parker's court. A fact that Bass Reeves knew only too well. Bass had seen many a man die on the gallows outside the Fort Smith courthouse. The feet of the condemned men would jerk, once, maybe twice, then stillness.

Bass walked down the streets of Fort Smith, Arkansas—a tall powerfully built man, he cut a striking figure. His dark bronze face was a mask of concentration as thoughts of the upcoming trial filled his head. How had he come to this? His life now hung in the balance, for he, Bass Reeves, was on trial for cold-blooded murder. He allowed that he had "shot" the man, but to call it "murder?" Bass had always considered himself to be unyielding on the right side of the law, the just side. He had never imagined that his life would depend on twelve jurors.

The events leading up to the man's death played over and over in Bass' mind. There were so many things he could have done to avoid it. But there was no sense reconstructing it in his mind. The deed was done. Bass shivered, though the night was not cold for an Arkansas October. His thoughts were on the past, back on the plantation, where he spent his early years. He was hearing the words of an old slave woman named Reba. She had predicted his future. She had told Bass' mother, Paralee:

> *"This boy child of yours, have a care. He ain't no ordinary field hand like most. He held as a child now, folkses laugh. But I been watchin' him, and listen'. His mind is runnin' ahead. He's gon' see greatness, and he gon' see danger, and he liable to die afore his time. But he got the restless. He cain't hep hisself. Others gon' make him a leader. Watch where he step if you want him grown to manhood."* [1]

If the jury came back with a guilty verdict all of the old woman's prophecy would come to pass. For surely, hanging would certainly cause him to *'die afore his time.'*

So preoccupied was Bass with the words of old Reba, that he didn't see the man standing in front of him. The tip of a walking stick jabbed into Bass' shoulder and he heard the words, "You damned Black son-of-a-bitch!" It took a second for Bass to recognize the man, but then he knew who he was.

CHAPTER **ONE**
Born in Bondage

The Republic of Texas was not yet a state when Paralee and Arthur (the future parents of Bass Reeves) arrived. They came separately—she a young slave girl, arriving with her newly married mistress, he a former slave, now a free man.

Paralee's young mistress was the bride to Master Stewart, an up and coming plantation owner besotted with his new wife. There apparently was no question as to whether he would allow his wife to bring Paralee, her lifelong companion and slave, with them to Texas. As a very young child, Paralee had been taken from her mother (Lucy Totty) and "given" to the young mistress as a companion. The two girls grew up together and were inseparable. Because she was her constant companion, Paralee was privy to all of the Bible stories that her mistress was taught. The Bible stories that she learned as a child would one day stand her in good stead. In secret, the young slave girl memorized the verses and passages of the Bible. Slave owners generally prohibited religious teaching, mainly out of fear that 'church' meetings would provide the opportunity to plot insurrections. The only lessons allowed were those that spoke of obedience, hard work, and thanking God for such "good" masters.

Paralee chose the Christianity that provided strength and offered relief from suffering. Her life, like the lives of countless African Americans in bondage, was indelibly marked by those who gave no thought to the impact their decisions would have on a young slave girl. In later years (Granny) Paralee always spoke fondly of her mother. A slave's life was dictated by her owners. The news that she would leave her mother and the only home she had ever known must not have come as a surprise. Regularly children were torn from their parents and sold. There could have been some comfort in the familiar presence of her mistress. Although on the long journey from Tennessee, Paralee may have had to make do with just herself for company. After all, it was a honeymoon of sorts for the newlyweds.

What must her fears and hopes have been? Did she ever dream of having a man to love her? Did she dream of children, and if she did, was it more a dream of fear? For bearing children in slavery meant bearing a child that you could not protect, could not perhaps even raise. The questions and fears in the young girl's mind were many. The familiar duties that she performed for her mistress would change as well. Would she be expected to take on the care of the master? The idea was frightening. Paralee's relationship with Stewart could be a living hell. She knew only too well that he could demand anything of her. For the moment he appeared to have no interest in her, except that she continue to wait on his wife. For that, Paralee was more than thankful.

Arthur Reeves was much luckier than Paralee. The decision to move to Texas was his to make. A free man, he controlled his own destiny, as much as any free Negro could in the early 1800s. Arthur was former wagon driver on the Santa Fe Trail. He came to the area as a freighter, delivering supplies and equipment to the settlements. Freedom for Arthur was precious. A self-confident man, Arthur viewed his freedom as a God-given right. For Arthur, slavery was a sin against God. Though illiterate, he had a good working knowledge of the Bible. He saw the contradictions between Christian law and man-made law. For him the laws of man that enslaved human beings were wrong. It is not clear exactly how Arthur gained his freedom. It is, however, clear that Arthur credited Benjamin H. Reeves with helping him obtain his freedom. In honor of his benefactor, he took the surname Reeves. History tells us that Benjamin Reeves was one of three commissioners appointed to survey the Santa Fe Trail.

The Santa Fe Trail began in Missouri and ended in the magical city of Santa Fe. The trail was primarily a business route. Merchants, tradespeople, Indians and adventurers all plied the route. Danger along the Santa Fe Trail came in the form of rugged terrain as well as resentful Indians. Peaceful treaties had been drawn by the commissioners and signed by the Indians though peace did not always reign on the Santa Fe Trail. Whites began aggressively hunting the buffalo, the Indians' primary source of sustenance. Often it was survival of the fittest. One had to be strong, healthy and quick-witted to survive the rigors of the Santa Fe Trail. Arthur Reeves was all three. What he learned on the trail can only be surmised. He must have dealt with Indians at some point. Whether he traded peacefully with them or fought ambushes along the trail is not known. In any event, Arthur Reeves was a well-traveled man, whose experiences were unique for a man of his color in the 1800s. It was with this background that Arthur Reeves came to Texas.

How the couple met is lost to history. That Arthur was welcomed on the Stewart plantation is a fact. Not much attention was paid to the free Black man that frequented the plantation. Otherwise, it would have been noted that the self-assertive and filled-with-himself Arthur was certainly out of place. To the unaware Stewart, the relationship between Arthur and Paralee could serve to increase his wealth since any children from the union would belong to him.

An additional bonus that came with the ownership of Paralee was her beautiful voice. Many a formal dinner ended with entertainment by young Paralee. Dressed in her mistress' cut-down dresses, Paralee would provide the evening's entertainment with song. She memorized all of the popular songs of the day as well as made up some of her own. On one occasion, the hem of her dress caught fire as she sang too close to the fireplace. Exhibiting the composure of a seasoned performer, she continued to sing, dancing around the room until the fire was out.

Arthur and Paralee never married, slave marriages at the time were illegal. (Slaves had no right to contract.) However, the bond between the two was strong. Little did they know that their union would provide the west with a formidable protector and a champion of justice.

**

About 1839 in northeast Texas, not far from the Red River, Bass Reeves was born.* He was the first and only son of Paralee and Arthur. His birth increased the wealth of Master Stewart and increased both the joy and fears of his parents. Named after Paralee's father Bass Washington, the baby boy brought to his father's mind the cruel facts of slavery. Here was a son Arthur

---

*Ordinarily slaves took on the surnames of their masters following a change in ownership. Out of respect for his father, Bass chose the name Reeves. The only surname Paralee was known to use was Stewart.

could be proud of, a son he wanted to raise to manhood, teach how to be a man. But in actuality, here was a son he could not claim nor protect, a son whose life was the property of another man. For Arthur it was a harsh reality. Arthur became more involved with people who could offer him hope. Hope of raising his son as a free man. Hope of being the head of his household. It was no surprise that Arthur Reeves aligned himself with those who would abolish slavery.

In February of 1840, slaveholders and plantation owners in the Republic of Texas were becoming more alarmed with the increased talk of freedom for slaves. Anti-slavery sentiment was growing stronger. Unlike the total oppression in the Deep South, slavery in Texas met staunch resistance, primarily from free Blacks. On the other side of the coin, slaveholders were determined to maintain the status quo. Shortly after the Texas Revolution broke out, the provisional government banned the immigration of free Negroes. Previously the law provided that those who were free at the time of Independence could stay, "as long as they choose." That law gave way to the pressure brought on by slaveholders who feared the rising anti-slavery sentiment. The recent action of banning Free Negroes from the area was taken to placate those who claimed that the presence of free Negroes led to the:

Infusion of dissatisfaction and disobedience into the brain of the lowest and contented slave.[1]

Of this, Arthur was a major offender. He spoke out against slavery to any Negro who would listen. Under the new law, free Negroes (those already in residence) were given two years to leave Texas or risk being sold into slavery. Even local Negro Revolutionary War heroes were targeted—the same men whom the Texas Congress had recognized as "among the first to shed their blood in the War of Independence." White veterans, who had fought 'shoulder to shoulder' with the Negro soldiers, vehemently opposed the new law, but to no avail.[2] The law was upheld.

Arthur and other free Negroes languished under a "veil of uncertainty" as successive legislatures proposed changes in the law. Arthur became more vocal in his indictment of slavery.

Oblivious to the freethinking Negro that frequented his plantation, Stewart continued business as usual. It appeared that Stewart was not threatened by Arthur's presence. Or perhaps he was not aware of Arthur's outspoken reputation. The popular thinking of the day was that a slave could not possibly be a threat to a White man. It was a way of thinking that was about to change.

While legislators argued the merits of allowing free Negroes to live in the state, little Bass spent precious time close to his mother, oblivious to the impending laws that would profoundly affect his life. Quieter than most children, Bass seemed to understand that his path would be different. Placed on the floor, he would sit and watch those around him as if memorizing everything he saw. Most of the time Bass was cared for by Reba, an elderly slave woman. When he was not with Reba, he could be seen toddling around after his mother as she went about her chores. For a time, peace reigned on the Stewart plantation. However, beyond the confines of the plantation trouble brewed.

**

Although Arthur faced a death penalty if found guilty of insurrection or any attempt to incite an insurrection, he was unable, or unwilling to curb his anti-slavery actions. He was in a race against the changing law and political climate. Meanwhile, his family grew with the birth of a daughter, Janie, Arthur spent more and more time on the plantation with his family. In the evenings when slaves were allowed to tend to their own lives, Arthur would listen as Paralee repeated the Bible stories she had learned with Mistress Stewart. Paralee was intent on teaching her children the Word of God. The salvation promised in the Bible was at times the only thing that gave her hope, the only thing that abated her fears. Arthur's stories were of a different nature, they were of Indians, herds of buffalo, mountains, rivers and long wagon trains. Young Bass' imagination was fueled by his father's tales of adventure. These stories he learned from both parents would stay with him for the rest of his life.

In 1845 Arthur's freedom was definitely no longer protected by law. In that year Texas gained statehood and came under the jurisdiction of the Federal Fugitive Slave Law. The law was designed to restore property rather than safeguard the rights of free men. Arthur and other free Negroes residing in Texas became fair game. Any free Negro could be deemed a slave under the revised law. The only evidence to prove that a Negro was an escaped slave was the sworn statement of a White man claiming ownership. The alleged fugitive could not defend himself, because he was explicitly prohibited from testifying in his own behalf. Slave catching became a national activity.

Arthur spent several anxiety-ridden years before making an agonizing decision. Though he was well known, all a slave catcher had to do was kidnap him and take him out of the area. Once out of the county, it was a simple matter of the White man swearing that Arthur was his escaped property. Arthur must have witnessed many a responsible and industrious man sold into slavery. Certain that his days as a free man were surely numbered, Arthur decided to leave Texas and his family. It was not an easy decision. His choices were intolerable. Stay and almost certainly lose his freedom, or go and leave his 10-year-old son and 7-year-old daughter, perhaps forever. After agonizing over his choices, it became clear that staying was not an option. Accounts of other free men who had disappeared or been outright kidnapped reached Arthur's ears. His only hope was to leave, make enough money to return for his children and Paralee. Even that was a fragile hope.

Pushing the doubts to the back of his mind, he gathered his children and tried to explain why he was leaving. For Bass it was a harsh blow. He was proud to have a father, and a free one at that. It was a source of pride to have a father who was free, one who was not like the other Negroes on the plantation. Bass wanted to go with his father, ride free with him. Arthur tried as best he could to explain to his son. Arthur might have been tempted to flee with his family, but reason prevailed. Slaves who tried to escape and were caught were killed, beaten or mutilated in some way. Taking his family with him greatly decreased their chance of success. Amid tearful goodbyes and promises to return, Arthur Reeves took his leave. His destination was California, he had heard the stories of gold being found there. He would strike out for his old stomping grounds and then on to California. If there ever was a man who needed to strike it rich, it was Arthur Reeves.

For young Bass it was his first hard lesson on the power of the law. He could not grasp how his father, who was free according to the law, could also be sold into slavery because of the law. This concept of the law was confusing for Bass. Fear and anger fought for attention in the young boy's mind. He shared his father's feelings about slavery, and now he was just as bitterly opposed to the law. Both had cost him his father. The resentment and anger that he carried inside worried his mother. So ingrained were the father's views in the boy that Paralee feared for his life. That much anger in a slave boy could only mean disaster.

As Bass grew he was placed in the fields with other boys. Young slaves usually began their work in the cotton fields pulling weeds and picking up scrap cotton left behind by the cotton pickers. Working up and down the rows of cotton, the young boy carried on a conversation with himself and anyone who was within earshot. He talked about guns and knives, and violent acts, even killings. Talk conducive to lynching. Word traveled back to Paralee about her son's obsession with violence. She was particularly troubled because he was so young to have so much of the seething rage that possessed his father. Paralee sought to calm her son, lest she lose him too. A woman of strong Christian faith, she believed that her young son could find relief in the teachings of Jesus. She doubled her efforts to teach Bass and Janie the Parables of Jesus and His concern for those who were unfairly treated and had no place to turn for help. A shrewd woman, she placed particular emphasis on the Biblical passages that told of the promises made to those who put their trust in God, the father of us all. That He who cares for the lilies and sparrows must care so much more for His children. A favorite Bible story was the story of Moses and the children of Israel.

Still Bass remained troubled. Word among the slaves was that he was destined for whippings, maybe even, hanging. Paralee had tried to turn her son's mind from the violence and the anger. Desperate, she turned to Reba, who was known for her mystical powers and her ability to read the bones. Reba did have a message for Paralee:

> *This boy child of yours, have a care. He ain't no ordinary field hand like most. He held as a child now, folkses laugh. But I been watchin' him, and listenin'. His mind is runnin' ahead. He's gon' see greatness, and he gon' see danger, and he liable to die afore his time. But he got the restless.' He cain't hep' hisself. Others gon' make him a leader. Watch where he step if you want him grown to manhood.*

Paralee shivered in the hot July night and pleaded, "Can't you tell me more? Somethin' to put my foot on?" The old soothsayer swept the bones behind a loose board, then replied: "Bones 'spect you to do the watchin'. Maybe later on I be's moved. I'll let you know. Jes' watch out for the master."

Paralee was startled. "But the master ..."

"That's all," said Reba puffing on her pipe, "Jes' heed the signs."

Heartened by Reba's prophecy Paralee determined that her son would not die before his time. She did not know if he would see greatness or become a leader. All that she did know was that Bass would grow to manhood if she had anything to say about it.

Under Paralee's firm guidance, Bass became less agitated and learned to control his anger and resentment. This was a valuable lesson for the young boy, a lesson that would serve him well in life. His concern for his mother was the driving force in his decision to control his anger and his tongue. He knew that it pained her when he spoke of violence and repeated some of his father's sayings. In an effort to please his mother, Bass curbed his tongue and concentrated on the Bible stories she told. Though he found comfort in the Bible and never questioned his mother's simple faith, he still carried a burning need to be free.

CHAPTER **TWO**
Path to Freedom

Three years had passed since Arthur's departure and the near thirteen-year-old Bass was as big as a full-grown man and still growing. Part of his job was providing water for the slaves who worked in the fields. His muscles strained as he toted the heavy buckets of water down the long rows of cotton. His mind wandering, Bass thought of the stories that his mother told him and Janie each night. The stories from the Good Book seemed to ease his soul. He still prayed nightly for his father, but now the prayers were different. He no longer prayed for his safe return, instead he just prayed for his safety. Even in his child's mind, he somehow knew his father would never return to the plantation.

He was old enough to understand the reality of the situation. He'd heard enough about lynchings to understand that coming home probably meant his father's death. Besides there were many other terrible ways a man could die traveling alone.

Reaching the end of the last row, Bass headed for the water trough. He liked this part of the day best. It was time to water the animals. He tended the mules and horses as if making a love offering. Bass was able to soothe his troubled spirit when he watered the animals. He spoke to them in quiet tones. It seemed as if the animals found comfort in Bass' presence as well. Stubborn mules, and skittish horses became calm and did the bidding of the teenager. Soon the word on the plantation was that if you wanted to get a stubborn animal to do something, call for Bass. Some said he could talk "horse-talk." Bass allowed himself to dream that one day he would have a stable of his own.

Having no clue that the slave boy dreamed of freedom, Stewart encouraged Bass' work with the animals. He recognized that Bass had a natural way with the horses. It was not long before Bass was taken from the fields to become the blacksmith's helper in the stable. Because Bass was swift with his work at the forge and eager to offer extra assistance, the blacksmith never grumbled when he spent extra time with the master's prize horses. Working in the stable was a step up for Bass. He was very tall, with hands so large that he could easily pick up a melon with one hand. His muscles began to catch up with his mind and his height. As each day passed, Paralee was reminded more and more of Arthur. Bass was growing up to be a powerfully built man just like his father. Arthur also had large hands with which he handled the many reins necessary to control unruly horses and mules on long arduous trails.

Bass remembered his father's stories about the Santa Fe Trail. How it felt to get paid for your work. Though freedom was always uppermost in his mind, he knew that he could not leave his mother and sister behind. The young man fervently believed that like the Bible stories his mother told him, one day they would all be delivered from bondage. Though sometimes it puzzled him that the mistress talked with his mother about all those stories. He thought that she ought to feel bad that she and the master acted just like the wicked people in the Bible. There was a lot he didn't understand, but he did understand that God's law was the right one. In all the Bible stories, the wicked perished and the righteous inherited the earth.

Though still slaves, Bass and his sister Janie enjoyed an easier life than the other slaves on the plantation. Paralee counted herself lucky that both of her children held prime positions on the plantation. To add to her contentment, Bass was chosen as the master's companion. That meant he had jumped several rungs up the ladder (as much of a ladder as slaves possessed). Bass was not the only one in his family to achieve a coveted job. His sister Janie's talent was with cloth, needle, and thread—a talent which earned her a position as seamstress on the plantation. At an early age, it became apparent that Janie had a knack for repairing torn garments. She moved from repairs to alterations. It probably fell on her shoulders to alter the mistress's hand-me-down gowns for her mother. In keeping with her brother's new station, Janie was called upon to 'tailor' Bass in clothes befitting the personal servant of the master. Janie made garments for many of the people on the plantation, both Black and White alike; nevertheless she paid close attention to her brother's outfits. It was a source of pride for Janie that Bass always looked his best.

Paralee was pleased with her son's improved status. Both of her children were close by, and they all ate from the 'house table.' At times seated around the table, Reba's warning seemed far off and not at all related to Paralee or her son.

Life for Bass continued to improve. He accompanied his master nearly everywhere, as valet, bodyguard, coachman and butler—all light duties compared with fieldwork, smithing, and stable tending. Traveling with Stewart brought Bass in close contact with a variety of White people. He was able to study the way they talked and behaved. His language skills improved as he learned more words. To help him understand the meaning of a word, he listened to its sound and watched closely the reactions of those conversing. He found that he had a knack for memorizing. His curiosity was aroused. He enjoyed the learning process and wanted more knowledge. There were books and newspapers present in the master's house. Bass knew that they contained a wealth of information. Innocently, he asked his master if he could learn to read some of the books and magazines that arrived from the East. Stewart adamantly refused. No slave of his would ever learn to read!

Stewart reflected the deep-rooted fears of most slaveholders. Reading meant knowledge, and knowledge led to power, and power could not be allowed, lest a slave use it for his own good. Demonstrating the contradictions of the times and his indulgence, Stewart did, however, allow his trusted slave, the use of his guns for hunting. To Stewart knowledge was a far more powerful and dangerous thing than a firearm. Stewart's decision regarding reading had a profound effect on Bass' life. He never learned to read or write, but the use of his master's guns would prove to be closely tied to his destiny.

Guns had always held a fascination for Bass, perhaps stemming from his father's tales of adventure. He was excited with the prospect of developing his skill. Surprisingly, he had easy access to the guns and shot. It was soon apparent that the young slave had a good eye and quick hands. This talent gave Bass a sense of self-confidence. He became an excellent marksman, easily surpassing his master who was himself a poor shot. Stewart was not concerned or intimidated with Bass' prowess with a gun. On the contrary, the amused master took pride in Bass' growing reputation as a marksman, and entered him in turkey shoots and other trials by firearms. In Stewart's mind,

Bass' ability with a gun was merely an extension of Stewart's persona. In addition, the young teen's skill ensured that the Stewart household was always stocked with fresh game.

Organized hunts were routinely held. The best horses and dogs were used. Bass thoroughly enjoyed these hunts, especially when he was called upon to shoot. Slaves using guns was not looked upon as anything out of the ordinary. They used guns to hunt and to protect livestock from predators that roamed the wild Texas countryside. However, this lax attitude towards slaves and guns was about to change.

Trouble was erupting in the west. In 1855 abolitionist John Brown launched anti-slavery activities in Kansas. A year later a wave of slave unrest swept across north Texas. While no actual physical relationship was established between Brown's exploits and the slave unrest several hundred miles to the south, his influence undoubtedly inspired many slaves to press for their freedom. In any case, the burning desire for freedom most definitely raged in Bass Reeves.

In 1857, despite an outbreak of plantation burnings, well poisonings, escapes and murders, the Texas House of Representatives' Committee on Slaves and Slavery reported:

> *Our slaves are the happiest three millions of human beings on whom the sun shines.*[1]

Local newspapers, however, disclosed what the state government refused to acknowledge. The Galveston News {January 17, 1857) reported:

> *Never has there been a time in our recollection when so many insurrections, or attempts at insurrection, have transpired in rapid succession as during the past six months. The evidence in regard to some of these has indeed proved very unsatisfac-*

tory, showing nothing but that the Negroes had got hold of some indistinct and vague ideas about obtaining their freedom ... In other cases, the plans have been more matured and in some instances, arms have been provided and all the necessary arrangements made not only to effect their own escape but to slaughter their owners.

The *Matagorda* (Texas) *Gazette* of September 12, 1860, carried the story of a meeting of slave owners in Marshall, Texas (the general area in which Bass lived). At the meeting a local man was convicted of being an abolitionist, and as a result, the slave owners asked Congress to make abolitionism an act of treason. In Fanning County, the newspaper reported three slaves hanged for killing their masters. The Gazette also stated that a mob of almost 500 hundred persons lynched a White man, "charged with having endeavored to incite the slaves of Wood, Titus and Hopkins Counties of an insurrection."[2] Fanning and Titus counties were in the region of the Stewart plantation.

The Biblical story of God delivering the Israelites from slavery deeply impressed Bass. More and more he was obsessed with the idea of his own freedom. Surrounded by unrest, he envisioned his own escape to the land of Kansas where people were fighting to be free. Still his mother and sister were uppermost in his mind. Concern for their well-being kept Bass on the plantation though his anti-slavery sentiments were becoming harder to ignore. Eventually, the amicable relationship between Bass and his master began to deteriorate. Increasingly the young manservant became more involved with the abolitionist movement. Traveling with his master, Bass acquired a thorough knowledge of the people and local conditions in the surrounding countryside. He passed the information on to those who planned escape routes and plotted insurrections. Even Stewart, the mild-mannered master, became aware of the political climate that surrounded him and threatened his way of life. A confrontation with Bass was inevitable. However, before the relationship deteriorated completely, fate stepped in.

Granny Paralee often told the story of the fateful day when Bass was sent to town on a routine errand. When he failed to return at the usual time, Paralee and Janie became alarmed since they knew that he often used the occasions to meet with others in the struggle for freedom. Janie, aware of her brother's anti-slavery activity, feared the worst. She tried to allay her mother's fears as best she could.

Late that night, heavily armed White men (men that Granny Paralee called 'paterollers') returned Bass to the plantation bound, beaten and bloodied. Paterollers were part of a patrol system formed to regulate slave conduct. It was obvious that a violent struggle had taken place. The 'paterollers' let Stewart know that Bass was returned alive only in deference to him. The men left the plantation assured that Stewart would handle the manner appropriately. Bass was put in an empty cabin while his fate was decided. Some family members have the master entering the cabin early the next morning and being overpowered by Bass. However, one family member, Aunt Nettie Robinson (Janie's daughter) surmised from talking with Granny Paralee and Janie, that a confrontation did not actually occur. She concluded that the master had gone to the cabin to actually assist in Bass' escape as he was convinced that Bass would surely hang. This reasoning is supported by the fact that Paralee and Janie remained on the plantation for a number of years without any reprisals whatsoever. Given Aunt Nettie's version, it is possible that the following occurred in the small cabin between master and slave.

Waiting until his wife fell into a fitful sleep, Stewart pulled his boots on and tucked his nightshirt into his pants. He made his way to the cabin. He stopped in front of the cabin door. He raised his lantern and unhitched the crude lock that had been placed on the door. When he stepped into the room, it seemed empty. He inhaled deeply, thankful that Bass had escaped. A noise halted his exhale. Turning slowly, he came face to face with Bass. For the first time in his life, Stewart looked at a Negro and felt fear. He had not realized how tall and how powerfully built Bass was. Stewart looked down at the broken twine hanging around Bass' wrist. Bass looked his master in the eye. He had no fear. Stewart glanced around the cabin. It was empty, safe for himself and Bass and the lantern he held. He hadn't brought a gun or whip with him. He had never needed one on his plantation. Now, the stories of plantation owners murdered in their beds came unbidden into his head. Both men remained where they stood. Bass finally spoke, "I don't want my Mama see me hanging from a tree." Stewart could only nod. He knew that at that moment he was not in control. Bass continued, "I'm a leave out of here fore day. What you gonna do to Mama and Janie?" Stewart shook his head slowly. "Nothing." Bass nodded his head. As Stewart returned the gaze, a flash of the young toddler playing on the kitchen floor ran through his mind. Nodding, Stewart backed out of the cabin. He closed the door and walked slowly back to the house.

What actually took place in the cabin was never known. On the subject of his escape, Bass was silent, neither denying nor verifying either version. What is known is that no reprisals were ever taken against Paralee or Janie.

Bass had long ago promised his mother that he would stay with her. However, the circumstances had made that promise impossible to keep. Paralee understood that he must go and go at once.

CHAPTER THREE
Freedom

Bass was a free man, he had secured food, other provisions, guns, and two of his master's prize horses to dash north across the Red River into Indian Territory. With two horses, he could cover more ground at a much faster pace since only one horse would tire under his weight. Bass rode until dawn then stopped and watered the horses. His heart was pounding so fast he wanted to jump back on the horse and ride. He rode hard, trying to put as much distance between himself and the Stewart plantation as he could. Hunkered down low on the horse, his bruised and beaten body was almost one with the animal. The wind stung the cuts on his face. It was a bittersweet pain—he was free!

The runaway followed the main trails through the Choctaw and Chickasaw Indian Nations to the Canadian River. Then he followed the river north, avoiding travelers and bypassing settlements and small towns when possible. Bass aimed his sights on the land of Kansas where there was no slavery.

The lonesome hours on the trail and the quiet nights gave Bass plenty of time to turn things over in his mind. He sorely missed his family and the only surroundings he ever knew. Traveling with his master had been enjoyable and he learned something new on each trip. Although this flight was different because deep within he savored the feeling of being free and began to realize what freedom really meant. He was no longer someone else's property but was his own man, accountable only to God. Besides, in this vast open land, a gun and a horse mattered more than what he had been or where he came from. He had never personally known any Indians. Bass knew the Indians were neither Black nor White and came from a far away place to live in this land. Meeting some along the way, he found them cordial and willing to help direct his route north. Others watched him from afar. None interfered with his bid for freedom. The beautiful rolling hills and dense woodlands with an abundance of game could indeed become his Promised Land. Thus did Reba's prophecy continue to unfold in 1857.

***

The Indian Removal act of 1830 forcibly removed thousands of Native Americans from their homes in the Southeast, forcing them to settle on the western frontier. Their new home was named the Indian Territory. The tragic journey of the Indians on their western march, "the Trail of Tears," took a heavy toll in lives and caused immeasurable suffering. Approximately 60,000 Indians were forced from their homes. In total five tribes were relocated, the Cherokee, Chickasaw, Choctaw, Creek, and

Seminole. Before they were forced from their homeland, many members of these tribes had adopted the dress, mannerisms and lifestyle of White settlers, causing the tribes to be known as the "Five Civilized Tribes." Each tribe constituted a separate nation in the Territory, with its own system of constitutional government and highly effective court and school systems. Part of the promise of the Removal Act was that, within the Territory, Indians would be free to govern themselves without interference from Whites. Most of the White people to be found in the Territory were citizens by intermarriage or legally bonded and certified traders.

It was twenty-seven years after the Removal Act that Bass Reeves rode into the Territory. One day passed, one night, then the next. After the fourth day, Bass breathed a little easier. His skill with the guns kept him amply fed. Though each time he pulled the trigger, he feared alerting slave catchers. After about a week, unbeknownst to himself, Bass was near the farthest northwest point of the Territory. He was in the Seminole Nation.

Finally stopping in a Seminole town, Bass was surprised to find two stores, a schoolhouse, a sawmill and a blacksmith's shop. He noted the blacksmith's shop; there he would inquire about work. As he rode through town, Bass discovered that he was not the only Negro. Mingled among the Seminoles were both slave and free Negroes.

The Seminole and Creek Indians did not treat slaves in the same manner that White southerners treated their slaves. Slaves in the Seminole nations were treated with respect. Many of the Seminole slaves were literate. Indeed, Bass would soon learn that slaves were an integral part of Indian society, some kept government records for the Seminoles. Other slaves were bookkeepers and language interpreters. It was inside this mélange of people that Bass Reeves found a home and lifelong friends. Not only accepted by the Seminoles, he was greeted as a conquering hero. The Seminoles were very impressed with Bass' tale of escape and the fact that he brought with him prize horses. It was a case of, "*The enemy of my enemy is my friend.*"

The Seminole town was built around a central courtyard. The society consisted of both full-blood and half-breed Seminoles. Full-blooded Seminoles were tied to the traditional ways, they shunned the adoption of the White lifestyle. Keeping to themselves, they hunted, fished and raised crops, coming to town mostly to trade for supplies. Full-blooded women wore traditional multi-colored skirts and moccasins; the men wore moccasins, fringed buckskin leggings, homespun pants, shirts and bright scarves. Half-breeds and other Seminoles had adopted the White man's lifestyle of dress of boots, jackets and hats.

Word had spread and by nightfall, there was a large gathering to celebrate Bass' triumph over John Stewart. Although they didn't know Stewart personally, the Seminoles were happy to celebrate any defeat of a White man. The Seminoles, allegedly the least "civilized" of the five tribes, was the last tribe to go west because of a gallant fight forced removal from their homeland.

Bass was accepted into the Seminole Nation. He was proud to be there. Years later, he would tell his great niece, Ethel Burks:

> *They [Indians] was mighty good to me. And when they learned about me and those handsome Kentucky horses and fine guns, they carried on like I won a war against White folks. Most of all I was proud to gain their trust, cause they was such a faithful people.*

Bass learned the language and customs of the Seminole with the help of the other Negroes in town. His background of superstition and religion made it easy for Bass to understand the beliefs of his new neighbors. The backbone of the Indians' belief system was a reverence for all of nature. Indians believed that they were one with the earth, that all things were connected.

Many said that the rivers sang and the rocks danced. It was not a great leap for Bass having grown up with the predictions and mysteries of Reba. She had said he would be free, and he was. It seemed to him there was a connection between these people and people like Reba.

Bass' acceptance into the Indian society came with an obligation to live according to their laws. Enforcing the laws of the land were mounted Indian rangers, known as the Light Horsemen (Lighthorse). The Lighthorse enforced the law in the Indian Nations. Bass adopted the communal responsibility and high regard for the laws of nature and of the Indians. He learned that there were powerful men within each tribe, some leaders and others chiefs. To Bass, the Indian system of justice (based primarily on personal integrity and honor) was most impressive. An Indian's word was sacred. Jails were usually unnecessary. If a convicted criminal gave his word that he would appear at an appointed time for trial or punishment, he would. Even those condemned to death would appear without fanfare for their own execution.

With the skills he learned on the plantation, Bass supported himself by breeding horses and working as a blacksmith. It became necessary for him to keep track of the number of horses he had as well as the amount of money he sold a horse for. The former slave soon realized that he had a head for numbers. He could keep a running total in his head and compute almost instantly how much money he was owed. His business flourished because a good horse was a valuable commodity. The Territory was vast. As his business grew, the demand that Bass speak the language of the other Indian people increased. Bass found that he was a natural linguist, becoming fluent in Creek, Cherokee and Seminole. He could hold his own with the other tribes as well. Traveling with his horses, Bass learned the whole Territory "like a cook knows her own kitchen."

Bass Reeves and his string of horses became well known. He was certainly a familiar sight to the Lighthorse. During the course of time, they befriended him. The Lighthorse taught Bass how to recognize nature's telltale signs for tracking and stalking prey. He also learned valuable survival skills, including how to use a silent killer trap when he needed to avoid the sound of a gun. After several years, his skills rivaled those of his teachers.

Life as a freeman suited Bass. He had almost everything that he could want—everything except a place of his own and a family. When he traveled he kept an eye trained for a possible home. His urge to settle down grew stronger each day.

Bass found himself especially drawn to the land of the Creeks. The Creek Nation was located in the eastern part of the Territory, and it was some of the most beautiful land that Bass had ever seen. Streams meandered through lush bottomland, trees abounded offering shade from the sun and shelter in the winter. He could call this place home. On his visits to the Creek Nation, he became acquainted with an influential chief.

Chief Opothle Yahola was a rich, powerful man with a large settlement where he raised horses, farmed and conducted political activities. Bass and Yahola shared a healthy distrust of White people. Yahola had learned early to distrust the White man.

As a young warrior, Opothle Yahola had been sent to warn a corrupt Creek chief, William McIntosh, not to give away the Creek homeland in Georgia. The warning that the young Yahola had delivered was clear, sign the treaty under penalty of death. McIntosh ignored the warning and signed the treaty, sealing his own death. Government officials admitted that McIntosh had not been authorized by the tribe to sign the treaty. However, a treaty was negotiated that was no better than the one signed by McIntosh. The Creeks were forced to exchange all their prime land in the southeast for a tract of land in Indian Territory. Thus they were torn from their homeland and settled in the Indian Territory.

What struck Bass most was the fact that the Indian Territory was safe from White man's law. He knew of the government's promise that the land would always belong to the Indians "[a]s long as grass grows and rivers run." Bass thought that at last he had found a place where he could live in peace.

Yahola liked discussing his plans for his people with Bass. Many evenings were spent discussing the White man's law versus the Indian's law. Bass understood the need to obey the law. However, his understanding stemmed from his knowledge of the Indian system of justice. His life with the Indians, coupled with his deep-rooted faith in the Bible, had instilled a great respect for the law. Like his Indian friends, Bass Reeves' word was his bond. He knew that his destiny was tied to the Creeks. Indeed, it was not only the land or discussions with Chief Yahola that made Bass a frequent visitor to the Creek nation. There was another reason, a reason that made his heart beat faster, made a long trip seem but a short distance. Her name was Jinney. Jinney was a refined young woman of Negro, Indian and White blood. She had bright copper skin and long flowing Black hair that she often wore in a bun at the nape of her neck. A tall woman, her large eyes emphasized her keen features and high cheekbones. Jinney had been educated in the mission schools and now assisted Chief Yahola with various social activities. Bass liked to watch as she moved quietly throughout the settlement. She had a grace that he found soothing.

Bass and Jinney both wanted a home and a family. They were both God-fearing people, and with Yahola's blessing, they began to make plans for the future. However, fate stepped in and their plans were interrupted, it was 1861.

Before Bass could realize his dream, their lives were totally disrupted by momentous changes that moved a divided America toward civil war. Even inhabitants of the Indian Territory were sought out to support either the abolitionists or those who favored slavery. Since most of the government agents who administered Indian affairs were Southern sympathizers, and since Southern states sent delegations to the Indians to gain support, all of the civilized tribes became allies of the Confederacy. However, Yahola bitterly opposed the alliances and urged neutrality for the tribes.

The chief invited all tribesmen who wished to remain neutral to join him at his camp. Several thousand men, women and children, mostly Creek and Seminole, arrived at the encampment with an array of cattle, horses, chickens, and wagons laden with personal effects. They were accompanied by several hundred Negroes. This was not a band of renegades and outlaws, but a group of law-abiding people compelled to flee for their safety. Haunted by the fear of capture, Bass early on aligned himself with Chief Yahola's dissidents.

Confederate leaders were apprehensive about the large gathering and planned to attack the neutral camp. Yahola learned of the plans soon enough to move north toward the Kansas line, seeking protection for the women and children. The first Civil War engagements in the Territory resulted in defeat for the Confederates by neutral warriors as they moved northward. But, out-manned and out-gunned, they were finally overwhelmed. In the face of a fierce onslaught and a freezing blizzard, many men, women and children were killed while others fled in wild disarray. Survivors, arriving in Kansas, had suffered incredible hardships. Nearly 250 Creeks died shortly after their arrival and countless frozen limbs were amputated.

During the perilous journey, Bass had scouted the advancing forces. After the final defeat, he did not proceed to Kansas. He was aware of Yahola's deferred plan to clear out the Confederates so his people could return peacefully to their homes. Along with others, Bass remained behind to help prepare for a triumphant return.

Broken in health but dauntless in spirit, Opothle Yahola quickly met with Union Army officers and offered to lead a regiment of Indians back to the Territory. However, this was not to be. His advanced years and painfully weakened body did not allow him to continue. Chief Opothle Yahola died in 1862. He was laid to rest in an unknown grave in Osage County, Kansas. One historian observed:

> *Opothleyahola enjoyed an uninterrupted leadership of the Upper Creeks for 40 years. No man in their history so touched the hearts of his people. In him, they saw a reflection of themselves. They knew he sympathized with their sorrows and understood their aspirations. He surpassed all others in those attributes which the Indians felt common to them all.*[1]

Bass was deeply saddened by Chief Opothle Yahola's death, but proud to have known such a great leader. He was intent upon helping fulfill the chief's dream. Before the chief's death, federal authorities agreed on a plan for invasion of Indian Territory by Union Indians supported by other regiments. Before the invasion, Bass, in contact with Union scouts, was able to help recruit Cherokees for the Union cause. The Union force included two uniformed regiments of the former neutral warriors, the first Kansas Colored Volunteer Infantry Regiment, and White infantry and cavalry units from Colorado and Kansas. Bass joined them as they invaded the Territory in the Cherokee Nation, moving down the Grand River Valley from Kansas. After several victories, they took Tahlequah and Fort Gibson. Following the famous Battle of Honey Springs and other successful engagements, Fort Smith fell and major conflict in the territory was over.

In August of 1861, Major General John C. Freemont, commander of the Western Department, issued a proclamation that all slaves who took up arms for the Union would be free. President Lincoln was so outraged, he fired Freemont. Other generals, however, took up the call. In October 1861, Brigadier

James H. Love formed the First Kansas Colored Volunteers. They were the first Black soldiers to serve in combat during the war fighting in a battle near Butler, Missouri, on October 28, 1862. *The Leavenworth Conservative* (Kansas) newspaper reported, "The men fought like tigers, each and every one of them, and the main difficulty was to hold them well in hand." Bass was especially proud to fight with the Indians and the Kansas Volunteers. On the battlefield, he was an awesome foe; death was preferable to being taken back into slavery. Like Bass, most of the Kansas Volunteers were escaped slaves, who, now free themselves, were more than willing to fight to the death to end slavery. Although there is no official record, Bass later told of fighting in the battles of Cabin Creek and Honey Springs. At Cabin Creek on July 2, 1863, the Volunteers were part of the main assault body that drove back twenty-two hundred Texans and Indians who had been concealed in rifle pits across the creek. Two weeks later, they again engaged the Confederates at Honey Springs. After the battle as if to underscore the resolve of the Black troops, numerous sets of shackles were found among the ruins of the Honey Springs depot. Confederate prisoners reported that they had planned to use the shackles on the Black soldiers they captured—to return them back to the south.

After the pivotal battle at Honey Springs, Commanding General James Blunt singled out the colored volunteers for their courage and valor, saying they particularly distinguished themselves:

> *Their coolness and bravery I have never seen surpassed. Blunt later remarked: [I never saw such fighting as was one by that Negro regiment ... they make better soldiers in every respect than any troops I have ever had under my command. Their desertion rate was only seven per cent compared to the nineteen per cent White desertion rate.]* [2]

In early 1864, efforts were launched to move the Union refugees in Kansas back to their homes in the Territory. One wagon train made a procession of almost three miles; in addition, approximately 3,000 Indians traveled on foot. They joined an equal number already in Fort Gibson. When Bass arrived at Fort Gibson, he was immediately put to work as an interpreter and to assist at a large refuge camp. Known to both Indians and federal authorities, he was the ideal choice.

The specifics of how Jinney and Bass were reunited are lost to history. It is known, however, that she arrived at Fort Gibson with the other refugees from Kansas. There was much suffering and bitterness among the Indians, but extreme hunger and utter desolation were the most serious problems. There had been widespread destruction of homes, crops and livestock because renegades, guerrillas, and the troops of both armies plundered and stole at will.

Bass' employment at Fort Gibson was the first time that he or any family member had worked on a near-equal basis with White people. Pleased with the praise and respect he received, the experience supported his reason for rejecting widespread notions that White men should be respected by Black men simply because of their color. At the war's end, Bass had been free for nearly ten years, but his newly vested rights meant he now had the same status previously enjoyed only by White men. He looked for ways to improve his condition. He never sought the respect of all White men. However, he was pleased that some gave him his due, even in front of other White men.

***

The system for handling the Indian Territory after the war differed substantially from the way the Confederate states were treated. As a penalty for joining the South, the Federal government held that all of the Indian nations had forfeited their land

and treaty guarantees. As a result, land was surrendered by each tribe to allow various states to settle other tribes in the Territory. Also, rights of way were granted for constructing railroads. Added to the poverty and ruin of war, Confederate and Union factions struggled to control the governments of each Indian Nation. The decreased tribal strength allowed disorder and lawlessness to flourish in the Territory.

The Territory, like the former Confederate states, was occupied by Federal troops. They were of little help in maintaining order, however, because of their limited numbers and the necessity of containing those Indians who either refused to sign treaties or accused the government of violating those in effect. Many dissatisfied Indians chose to fight to stop White intruders from taking more and more of their land. Bands of raiding parties struck all along the frontier, and some tribes, including the Kiowas, Comanches, and Cheyenne, raided communities and stole cattle in the Territory.

To help stem these attacks, the new United States Ninth and Tenth Cavalry regiments were assigned to the region. The regiments had been organized in accordance with an 1866 Congressional act establishing six Black regiments in the U.S. Army.[3] *These Black troops*, dubbed "Buffalo soldiers" or Black White men . . . "were the scourge of the Plains Indians. They had literally nothing to lose and everything to gain by acquiring a good military reputation. Next to the Light Horsemen, they were the toughest, hardest-riding organized bodies of troops on the plains."[4] They served heroically as major forces in bringing peace and order to the western frontier. Bass had made many friends with the Tenth Cavalry when it was temporarily stationed at Fort Gibson. While he was continually urged to join, he was now filled with the exhilarating air of freedom. Though the army offered former slaves a secure job, a place to live, food, shelter and clothing, plus a modicum of respect, it was not a life Bass wanted to live. To be told what he could do or could not do was a serious denial of his freedom, enlistment to him was simply out of the question.

CHAPTER **FOUR**
Mixed Blessings

The war was over and for Bass Reeves it was the beginning of prosperity. Not so for those who had been his neighbors, customers and friends, for them it was a time of mourning. The overall conditions in the Indian Territory had deteriorated dramatically. Just how much became evident as Bass helped interpreting during the initial meetings between the tribal leaders and the Federal government. Many of the Indian representatives could not understand or speak English.

The price the Indian Nations paid for siding with the Confederacy was high. Harsh punishment was administered for participation in a war that was not their own. The structured and lawful way of life that the Five Tribes had enjoyed prior to the Civil War was destroyed.

Bass struggled to find justice in the law. What he saw was the strength of each tribe undermined. He knew how important land and community were to the Indians. The punishment meted out to the Indian nations was far more severe than the punishment dealt to former Confederate states. Bass watched as a proud and orderly people were cast aside, their humanity discounted, and their land once again stolen. Many of the chiefs still believed in the treaties that they had once signed. They also believed that they could negotiate a better deal. To that end, Bass traveled with several Indians to Fort Smith, Arkansas, who met to draft new treaties.

The trip to Fort Smith was Bass' first out of the Territory since arriving nearly ten years earlier. He had entered the Territory a fugitive on a quest to gain his freedom. He now rode out of the Territory a free man. While in Fort Smith, Bass decided to use the occasion to visit Van Buren, Arkansas five miles down the Arkansas River.

The Indian nations and their respective courts had exclusive legal jurisdiction in all matters where Indians were the only parties. But jurisdiction over White persons rested with the U.S. District Court in Van Buren. Deputy marshals who policed the territory were also headquartered in Van Buren. The actions of the deputies regarding criminal offenses by or against Indians involving Whites were generally resented by the Indians.

Indians found themselves at a severe disadvantage, usually traveling great distances, they often faced a language barrier; in addition, the lack of knowledge of the White man's law and legal procedure exacerbated the situation. The simple knowledge that they had the right to produce witnesses on their behalf eluded most of the Indian population. Deputies often neglected to inform the Indians of any of their rights, due to either prejudice or lack of communication. With his extensive knowledge of the Territory and its people, Bass was confident that he could fill an obvious void by offering his tracking and interpretive services to the deputies.

Business was booming in the Van Buren court. The lawlessness triggered by the Civil War and the increased presence of Whites produced a large number of legal disputes. Deputy Marshals and bounty hunters had more than enough work to keep them busy and financially well off, a fact that was not lost on Bass.

Back in Fort Smith, with the meetings concluded, Bass and the Indian delegation headed back to Fort Gibson. Something weighed heavily on Bass' mind. Van Buren seemed like the next logical place for him. He had decided to relocate to the Van Buren area. But what of Jinney? Would she agree with him? More importantly, would she leave Fort Gibson? Jinney had been uprooted so violently the first time. It was a quiet ride back to Fort Gibson, each traveler lost in thoughts of what the future held for him.

Back in the Territory, it was as Bass had expected. Several Indian factions refused to recognize the new treaties. They accused the Federal government of violating the old treaties. In retaliation, Indian raiding parties terrorized law-abiding citizens. In addition to the Indian raiding parties, outlaws used the Territory as a sanctuary. Robbing banks, trains, and businesses in adjoining states, the criminals would flee to the Territory for cover. Federal troops that occupied the Indian Territory were of little help.

On arrival in Van Buren, Bass faced the expected obstacles. Though qualified manpower was sorely needed, the deputies and bounty hunters had no desire to work with Bass. A Black man was not someone they wanted to deal with on anything resembling an equal footing. However, it soon became apparent that indeed Bass had something they needed. It was not long before Bass established himself as a force in capturing outlaws.

It was often said in later years that Bass Reeves was a quiet man, not given to small talk. This trait could have had its start in

Van Buren where the men that he worked with kept their distance, mostly avoiding any unnecessary conversation with him. If they needed his help, they would talk to him, otherwise he was more often treated either as invisible or with contempt. Bass endured the shabby treatment, because he had plans that depended on his working out of the marshal's office. He kept to himself. This in itself proved to be another boon for him. He could learn a lot simply by listening to the deputies and bounty hunters. Most thought of him as nothing more than a convenience, a tool that helped get their jobs done. However, the perspective changed once they crossed the border into the Territory. On many occasions, the presence of Bass Reeves meant the difference between life and death. His knowledge of the Territory, his tracking skills and ability to communicate with the Indians became more important than the color of his skin. Work as a scout and tracker earned Bass reasonable sums of money. He also shared rewards with the bounty hunters that he assisted. Bass soon realized that he didn't need the bounty hunters to capture a fugitive. Posters in the Marshal's office, referred to as 'dodgers,' bore the likeness of the wanted criminal, his crime, and the amount of the reward offered for his capture, and Bass understood figures.

On the occasions when he brought a wanted man in on his own, he made considerably more money. The obvious question must have crossed his mind. Why share a reward with someone when he did most of the work? Bass began to concentrate on fugitives that he could capture by himself. With the capture of each fugitive, he moved one step closer to the dream of owning a horse farm.

Because of the number of criminals swarming in and around the Territory, Bass realized his dream sooner than expected. Not long after the Civil War ended, Bass was able to buy his farm and settle down.

The land Bass selected was ideal for the peaceful family life he wanted for himself and Jinney. The property included a spring-fed pond and several acres of grazing land. It was large enough for a corral for the horses and several houses. The plan was to build a house for him and Jinney, and then two more for the family he had left in Texas.

The years away from the plantation had not dimmed his memory of his mother and sister. He wanted them with him. His dream included settling his mother, Janie and the siblings that he had yet to meet, in Van Buren with him. It is not known how Bass managed to keep in touch with his family over the years. That he did, given the difficulty of the times and the fact that he could neither read or write is a testament to his strong commitment to family.

Bass returned to Fort Gibson and claimed his bride. Bass Reeves was embarking on his dream. For Jinney and Bass, it was an exhilarating time. Jinney had survived the persecution of her people during the Civil War. Bass had survived slavery and together they had endured much and accomplished a great deal. The past, however, still encroached on their present happiness. Originally, they had planned to settle in the Creek Nation. Had it not been for the war, they would be building their home on Creek land. Jinney would be surrounded by friends and relatives. Life was about the bitter and the sweet, sometimes coming at the same time. Bass remembered those far away days. Though it was different for him, he was used to life turning itself upside down. His world was constantly changing, from slave to fugitive, from fugitive to a respected member of the community.

Perhaps it was the stories of adventure that his father told him as a young boy, or maybe it was his mother's unshakable belief that the Lord would make a way. Whatever the reason, Bass Reeves was a man who was never afraid of the future, never doubted his ability, or his place in the world.

With the two other houses built, Bass sent for his mother and siblings. Janie was married by this time, and Paralee had two other children, John and Lucy Belle. There are no records showing that Paralee ever married. However, family history discloses that Paralee's youngest son, John Stewart, was the son of her former master, and Lucy Belle's father was Milton Gautier, a Frenchman by birth. Paralee, Lucy Belle (named after Paralee's mother), John, Janie, and her husband, John Brady, with their two children, moved to Van Buren. As luck would have it, John Brady was an excellent horse breeder from Tennessee. He was to become an immeasurable help to Bass.

The Reeves' property grew over the years. Bass enjoyed a happiness he could not have imagined a few years earlier. Horse breeding allowed him to travel and support his family. With the help of his brother-in-law, the farm grew prosperous. Life was good for Bass and his family, but not so for scores of Indians and Negroes left homeless after the war.

Bass knew that life was painfully oppressive for most Black folk in the area. He shared his fathers' strong belief in justice and human rights. Though Arthur Reeves was lost to him, his spirit and belief in the equality of all men lived in Bass' heart. Angered by the system of intimidation and chicanery that prevailed against the former slaves, Bass sought ways that he could help. It wasn't easy. Former slave owners controlled the local governments, they used the law to take advantage of their former slaves. Contracts and work agreements were devised to exploit and cheat the newly freed people. Negotiations for fair wages were out of the question, and the notion of sharecropping was born. Negroes were often given food and shelter in exchange for labor. They accepted either whatever work or wages offered or faced arrest for vagrancy, forcing them into the clutches of a new kind of slavery. Despite the dismal circumstances, Negroes drew strength from their families, extended families and the communities that they formed.

The Reeves' compound became a satellite for other former slaves. Many migrated to land near Bass and his family. It was not long before a thriving community was established.

Paralee was the matriarch of her family and a respected elder of the community. A devout Christian and still a strong and vibrant woman, true to form, Paralee recited her Bible stories to all that would listen. Soon regular meetings were held to talk about the Word of God. It was not long before the community realized that what they needed was a central place of worship, a church. Paralee joined other former slaves to build a church, a place where they could all worship as a free people. The pride and joy they all must have felt! Many had never been in a church before, still others had not dreamed that they would one day walk into the front door of a church built with their own hands.

In 1869 the Mount Olive Methodist Church was completed. It was a day filled with reverence and thanksgiving for the entire community. It was with great pride that Bass and his family stepped inside the sanctuary to worship for the first time. Sister Janie had made sure that everyone in the family was 'tailored.' Bass eventually became a deacon in the church. God had seen him through precarious times and saved him from the destructive anger he had felt when his father left. And now God had brought his family to Van Buren where they could attend their own church. God was indeed good. The building of the church was a singularly proud accomplishment in the history of Bass Reeves, his family, and his neighbors. Faith in God provided an immeasurable strength for many people as they struggled with their newfound 'freedom.' His worship was an important part of their lives. Mount Olive was a focal point of the community, providing not only a stirring message in sermon and song, but a fellowship that lifted their spirits and refreshed their weary souls. The Mount Olive Methodist Church stands today as a monument to those people who came out of slavery and carved a life for themselves. For one hundred and twenty years after the opening of the church, our family remained staunch members.[1] For the many years of devoted service, the church dedicated a stained glass window in memory of family member Arthur Brady (Janie's youngest child and the author's uncle).

All in all, it was a time of peace and prosperity for Bass and his family. The lawless conditions in the Territory seemed far away. Outlaws and raiding parties were elements that to many were only stories told to frighten children into minding.

True to Reba's predictions, Bass' mind was 'running ahead.' Despite his placid surroundings, his thoughts often returned to the free-roaming life he had known. He could not deny that deep down, *'the restless'* that Reba had warned his mother about was still with him. Though he was prosperous and his dreams seemingly realized, he found himself wondering if there was not indeed more for him to do. He knew that he should count his blessings. The life he led was truly a dream. Bass struggled to ignore the wanderings of his mind and concentrate on his farm and his family. However, destiny was not through with Bass Reeves. There were many more milestones to accomplish. Circumstances that at first glance had nothing to do with Bass Reeves would soon change his idyllic life.

***

Progress and commerce were barreling west. Plans for a rail line were under way. The line would run directly through the Territory, from the Kansas border north of Fort Gibson in the Cherokee Nation and south to Texas. Experience had taught government officials that they could expect trouble, lots of it. Bands of raiding parties still plagued the area. Outlaws roamed the land anxious for new targets, and railroad work parties were ideal targets for both. What was needed was protection, someone to act as an advance scout, someone who knew the lay of the land as well as the people. An official for the railroad remembered working with a man, a Negro, who would be perfect for the job.

***

Bass listened as the former army officer turned railroad official presented his case. He remembered working with the man at Fort Gibson. Bass listened patiently. The railroad company needed an advance scout for the initial survey crew. Bass' experience and connections would surely decease the amount of trouble they would encounter. As the man spoke, Bass could feel the 'old restless' stir. It was a tingling sensation that he recognized. It was also a feeling that he tried to ignore. Life for him was good, his family was well taken care of. At first Bass declined the offer. He was content to stay on his farm, traveling only when he needed to trade horses. Jinney also felt that Bass would be better off working for himself and not getting involved with White men. To her the Territory rightfully belonged to the Five Tribes. The Federal government had given the land to them and promised no interference from Whites, "[a]s long as grass shall grow and rivers run." The business with the railroad was just another direct violation of the original treaty. She wanted nothing to do with it.

Although Bass originally agreed with Jinney, there was something else that made the job offer very tempting. He could make money with the scouting job; and at the same time he could buy choice Indian ponies for his breeding stock. Bass' entrepreneurial spirit prevailed. Because he would be working in the Territory, he would have easy access to Indian ponies. Bass' thoroughbred lines were known for their size and strength. The Indian ponies were known for their speed and endurance. The combination would be highly profitable; breeding the two would produce horses that had the stamina and agility necessary for cattle work, and at the same time were excellent saddle mounts. For Bass, it looked like a win-win. He accepted the job, but there were stipulations. He wanted assurances that he would be fully respected as a member of the survey team and that he would in no way be looked on as a servant or less than any other man on the crew. He remembered all to well his treatment while working out of the Van Buren court. The railroad official quickly agreed. However, Bass must have known that there were no guarantees that everyone on the crew would comply. With the agreement in place, Bass joined the survey crew.

Along the way, he was amicably met by Indians, many of whom knew him or knew of him. His reputation and skill with the language helped pave the way for the survey crew. Bass enjoyed working with the crew, he was fascinated with the instruments that they used. A quick study, Bass learned how to use some of the survey equipment. One engineer gave him a 'spy glass' that he carried with him for many years.

With the survey complete, Bass prepared to head home. However, the railroad had other plans. Bass was asked to stay to help keep order as construction crews began laying track. By this time the restless in him had been quenched, but not entirely. Continuing to work in the Territory greatly appealed to him. Bass agreed and joined several ex-lawmen, hired to keep the railroad construction workers physically able to work and to protect supplies and equipment.

Company officials were impressed with Bass' physical ability and no-nonsense attitude, his presence cut down on the number of 'problems' among the workmen.

The end of the track posed an even greater challenge. The end-of-the-track was the construction supply area that moved as each leg of the roadbed was built. This was where the real trouble waited. Whiskey peddlers, prostitutes, and card sharks waited to fleece the railroad workers. Indians bent on blocking the railroad focused their attention at the end of the track along with thieves and killers. Federal marshals were ineffective in maintaining law and order. Their numbers were so small that the marshals could not follow the construction crew or remain at the end-of-the-track. Therefore, Bass and the other law enforcers hired by the railroad were, in effect, the 'law at the end-of-the-track.'

Working alongside Bass was a man named Arch Landon, a former U.S. Deputy Marshal. Bass and Arch worked well together. Each relied on the other in their efforts to maintain order. Though Bass was a crack shot with a rifle and shotgun, he was limited with a handgun. Landon offered to help his new friend hone his handgun skills. Bass readily accepted. Landon taught Bass that the key to handling a gun was to quickly get it into action and fire accurately. True to form, Bass spent almost every day practicing. His diligence again paid off. His prowess with a handgun soon rivaled his ability with the long guns. D.C. Gideon later noted, "Bass handled a revolver with the ease and grace acquired only after years of practice."

Bass always remembered Landon's advice for using a gun in close quarters because so often things happened fast. He had no problems learning the lessons taught him by Arch Landon. His life was in the balance. A false move born of ignorance could bring Reba's worst prediction into being. Bass practiced all that he learned, and kept a cool head, for the most part. Unlike the survey crew that Bass had worked with, the railroad construction workers were under no obligation to treat him with civility. In fact most of the time, his presence was clearly resented. Racial slurs were commonplace. Bass' patience was tried on too many occasions to count. There were times when keeping a cool head seemed a tall order indeed.

A favorite pastime of the men laying track was proving who was the biggest and baddest. Fights were an everyday occurrence. Breaking up fights and drunken brawls became routine for Bass. On many occasions, he had to knock out two or three men to keep the peace. This did not sit well with many of the workers. They had trouble adjusting to a Negro who walked with his head held high and carried a .44 Colt strapped to his hip. Bass' authority was questioned on a regular basis. Racial slurs were part and parcel of his existence at the end of the track. An eruption was bound to occur in the highly charged atmosphere.

The explosion came after Bass was subjected to a long jeering tirade that ended with loud mocking laughter. A burly tracklayer continued hurling racial slurs at Bass. It had been a long day, and perhaps Bass had heard the slurs one time too many. Suddenly the track worker found himself flat on his back. Bass had landed a powerful blow to the man's jaw, knocking him over backwards. Spitting blood and staggering to his feet, the railroad tough continued to hurl racial epithets. Bass unbuckled his gun belt and dropped it. He would fight the man and shut him up once and for all. With the absence of the gun the workers became bolder. This was an opportunity they had been waiting for. Now the crowd began talking loudly about what a Negro could and could not do to a White man. Bass waited for the loud-mouthed tough to throw the first punch, but instead, he found himself staring down the barrel of a gun. Someone had tossed it from the crowd. Before the gun could be cocked, Arch stepped out of the crowd and crashed the barrel of his gun on the railroad worker's head. The big man collapsed in a bloody heap. The fight was over before it began.

Bass had had many fistfights and brawls, but this was the most memorable. It was painfully clear that he could not expect a fair fight. He decided that he would not be goaded or moved to battle solely by anger or the need for revenge. Bass realized that even with a cool head, the latest episode was bound to repeat itself. Sooner or later, he would be forced to rely on his gun and gunplay could easily end in a killing. One killing would undoubtedly lead to another and perhaps another. Bass operated solely as an employee of the railroad company, he had no other legal authority to back him. The railroad might not attempt to justify his conduct before the law. Then, there was always the possibility of witnesses lying. The money and the procurement of Indian ponies were just not worth his life. He had a family to think of. The prediction of Reba echoed in his mind " ... liable to die a fore his time." Bass decided it would be best to devote himself to his family and breeding horses. He'd leave peace keeping to others. At least that was the plan.

CHAPTER **FIVE**
The Best Laid Plans

Most Indians had known nothing but trouble from their contact with the white man—from the beginning up until the present. Completely oblivious of the law, the outlaw element ran wild. Since the tribal courts were limited in their jurisdiction over the individual nations, they were not prepared to handle the crisis. To help deal with the increased White presence, Congress was prompted to act. Accordingly, on March 3, 1871, the United States District Court in Van Buren was moved to Fort Smith, a short distance up the Arkansas River on the boundary of the territory.

Fort Smith, the Border City of Arkansas, originated in 1817 when General Thomas Smith established a military post for protection against hostile Indians. Located at the junction of the Arkansas and Poteau Rivers, it was favorably situated as an important point for emigrants going to the Far West. Steamboats regularly landed from points as far away as Cincinnati and New Orleans. Growing steadily as a commerce and distribution center, Fort Smith's warehouses stocked merchandise to accommodate the brisk trade with Indians and White settlers for hundreds of miles around.

In 1875 the town was a volatile mix of cowboys returning from long cattle drives, river men, and railroad workers, all with money in their pockets and pent-up energy. It was described as a tough town. Although the population was less than 3,000, 30-plus saloons lined the streets, none of which ever lacked customers. Saloon owners were not the only people making their mark. Some local citizens concentrated on building churches, schools, and hospitals. Touches of culture were offered by concerts and other activities. Later the Grand Opera House would be constructed, bringing the best shows to Fort Smith. Nevertheless, for Bass and other Negro citizens, who lived in the area, life was far from pleasant. White supremacist notions were still alive and well ten years after the Civil War.

Presumably, slavery had been the dominant reason why Arkansas joined the Confederacy. On November 30, 1860, the *Van Buren Press* editorialized, "If certain southern states seceded, Arkansas would be forced to secede also, or abolish slavery. It is, of course, too great a pecuniary sacrifice to do the latter, she must adopt the former course." At a secession convention in May 1861, almost everyone in Fort Smith reportedly agreed that, "We will resist [Union policies] even to the death! And to this end, we pledge our fortunes and our sacred honor!"

Most of the Black population had been slaves in the area who left the fields to work in Fort Smith. Looking to improve themselves, they loaded and unloaded boats, transported cargo, and labored in warehouses. Others held menial jobs in hotels, saloons, and in private homes. Despite a continuing influx of southerners and strict racist policies, the Black people had faith that basic fairness would ultimately prevail under the recent Constitutional amendments that ended slavery and provided fair and equal treatment for all.

On occasion, when he went to Fort Smith, Bass visited his friends at the court. Although anxious to learn the latest news from the territory, it was invariably disheartening. The trips usually left him in a reflective mood, and in the words of the old slave woman, stirred "the restless" in him. But he was consoled with the thought that as a private citizen beholden' to no one, he had every right to live life without concern for the problems of others.

The worsening conditions in the territory were not only attributed to the outlaw element, but also to a deterioration of Federal law enforcement. Immediately after the Congressional action, President Grant appointed William Storey to the court in Fort Smith. Judge Storey, a weak man, allowed the court to become the subject of graft and corruption. Huge unexplained disbursements were made and often subpoenaed witnesses and jurors were unpaid, even forcing some to sell their horses and walk home. Storey, facing charges of bribery, resigned rather than risk impeachment.

It seemed that Storey was more interested in lining his pockets than eradicating crime. Although the punishment for breaking the law was clear, it was rarely enforced. Hanging was the fixed punishment for capital offenses. Two to 21 years at hard labor was given for arson. Assault with a deadly weapon brought one to five years hard labor. Horse stealing carried a maximum $1,000 fine and 15-year imprisonment. Obstructing railroads was punishable by hard labor of up to 20 years. Selling, trading or giving spirits or wines to Indians brought a $50 fine and a $1,000 fine for operating a distillery. In just over a year of Judge Storey's tenure, more than 50 murders were committed without subsequent arrests. Liquor flowed freely throughout the land.

The Indian nations were convinced that all had abandoned them. The Territory became known as the 'Robber's Roost' and the 'Land of the Six Gun.' A popular slogan of the day succinctly summed up the conditions in the Territory: "There is no Sunday west of St. Louis—and no God west of Fort Smith." "No American frontier ever saw leagues of robbers so desperate, any hands so red with blood." In 1875, four years after the court moved to Fort Smith "... civilization was in the balance. Decent men, Red and White alike, cried to the government for protection."[1]

Unbeknownst to many, change was just around the corner. A change that would not only affect the freewheeling outlaws, but a change that would also have a profound effect on Bass Reeves. The catalyst for change came in the form of one Judge Isaac C. Parker.

In March of 1875, President Grant appointed Isaac C. Parker to the Fort Smith court. For $3,500 a year, Isaac Parker was charged with literally cleaning up the 74,000 square miles of Indian Territory which included wild frontier stretching from Arkansas to Colorado and lying between Texas and Kansas. As a rule, judges were chosen from candidates within a state. Because of a political fight in Arkansas, known as the Baxter War, it was decided that an out-of-state appointee, not identified with either side, was acceptable. An honest and incorruptible outsider was needed for the court. Isaac Parker was such a man. Before his appointment, Parker had been a judge in St. Joseph, Missouri, from 1868 to 1870, then as congressman from 1871 through 1875. While in Congress, he sought to improve conditions relating to Indians through his work on the Committee on Territories. While serving on the committee, he sponsored the Indian Appropriation Bill of 1872. Parker also introduced a bill designed to give Native Americans civil government in their Territory. He was a perfect choice.

Upon his arrival, Isaac Parker found appalling conditions. The brick court building consisted of the courtroom and offices on the first floor, and cells were located in the basement. Prisoners were herded through barred doors into two large cells. The cells were a disgrace. Fifty to one hundred inmates occupied a room. Stone floors and walls of the cells made them cold in winter, damp in summer, and poorly ventilated during all seasons. Pails placed in the cells served as toilets. The pails were emptied only periodically leaving behind sickening odors. At the time of Parker's arrival, the press had described the jail as "A hell-hole of reeking filth ... better adapted to the fattening of swine, than the confinement of human beings." Though the condition of the jail was a concern, Parker had more pressing matters. He needed to quickly establish himself as a man who believed in the letter of the law.

Eight days after arriving in Fort Smith, on May 10, 1875 Judge Parker began his war on crime and opened his first court term. It was a busy first day. Eighteen people stood before him that day, all charged with murder. Fifteen were convicted and eight sentenced to die on the gallows. After pronouncing his first death sentence, he reportedly bowed his head and wept. The message sent that day was clear. Judge Isaac Parker was no William Storey.

One of Parker's first official acts was to swear in as his marshal, James Fagan. He then began appointment of the 200 deputies authorized by the Justice Department to enforce the law. Some observers, who knew the situation in the Territory, advised Judge Parker against assigning unfamiliar and often arrogant White men as deputies. The Territory was a foreign country to them. Most did not understand Indian people nor their customs. A good example of this was the 'Going Snake incident.'

In April 1872, a Cherokee Indian was on trial for murdering a fellow Cherokee in the Going Snake Courthouse (Cherokee Nation), clearly an Indian matter. Nonetheless, marshals entered the courthouse and attempted to take the defendant to Fort Smith for trial on another charge. In the ensuing gun battle, eleven men were killed, including seven of the Fort Smith group. The event nearly resulted in war and became known as the 'Going Snake Incident.'

Indians prized honor, courage and honesty above all other virtues. Parker understood this and agreed that, in order for a deputy to be effective in the Territory, he had to have the respect of the Indians. Parker sought recommendations from the court officials. They agreed that there was one man that fit the bill, Bass Reeves. In addition to having their trust, Bass' experience as a scout and tracker made him an ideal choice.

In the summer of Parker's first year in Fort Smith, he set his mind on persuading Bass to serve an indefinite term with his court.

Fate had once again stepped in. For the third time in his life, Bass was offered a job maintaining order. He had left the railroad job because he had been asked to perform a job that came with no legal authority. Now Judge Parker was offering him an opportunity to maintain law and order with the full backing of the legal system, a very tempting offer.

Bass found in Parker a kindred spirit. Both were devoutly religious and both held duty and honor in high regard. From the beginning, Bass believed that Parker was as much a friend to the Negro as he was to the Indian. Despite their widely diverse backgrounds, they developed a deep mutual respect for each other. Aunt Nettie often quoted Bass as saying that, while he admired the Judge's knowledge and intelligence, he respected most his dedication to "serving and doing justice."

In his effort to convince Bass to join his court, Judge Parker pointed out that Deputy Marshals were specifically authorized to enforce the recently enacted Civil Rights Act (March 1, 1875). Included were provisions that entitled all citizens to full and equal enjoyment of public accommodations regardless of any previous conditions of servitude. The two men indulged in frequent discussions about the meaning of the Constitution and its Amendments—Parker, the teacher, and Bass, the apt student. Parker explained the distinction between the rule of law and the arbitrary rule of powerful men. The rule of law stated that all men were equal before the law. Powerful men tended to pick and choose who would be equal, according to their own law. A practice Bass knew all too well.

Though they spent hours in conversation, Bass was reluctant to join the court. He shared his reservations about taking the job and putting himself at considerable risk because of the nature of the job and the color of his skin. The judge gave his word that Bass would be treated with only the utmost dignity and respect while serving his court. Parker also emphasized that cleaning up the west, establishing and maintaining law and order was something much bigger and more important than either one of them. If ever a man had a destiny to fulfill it was Bass. The prophecy of old Reba continued to unfold.

> ... *He's gon' see greatness, and he gon' see danger, and he liable to die afore his time. But he got the 'restless.' He cain't hep' hisself. Others gon' make him a leader. Watch where he step if you want him grown to manhood.*

Bass embraced the prophecy. That is all but the "he liable to die afore his time" part. Determined to fulfill his destiny, Bass tentatively agreed to become one of the first men "to ride for Parker." His goal was to establish order out of chaos in the land he had grown to love.

Bass considered the effect taking the job would have on his family. Jinney was his chief concern. Thus far the Lord had not blessed them with children. Accepting the job would keep him away from home a good deal of the time. Though he knew that Jinney was surrounded by family, he still worried. She was a homebody, her life centered on husband, home and family. It was asking a lot of her to bid him farewell, knowing that each day on the job could be his last.

Aware for sometime that her husband had 'the restless,' Jinney foresaw a total disruption of their peaceful farm life. Quiet by nature and adverse to complaining, her overriding love and respect for Bass helped her understand how deeply he believed in what he had to do. She had been told of the prophecies of Reba, the old slave woman. But Jinney already knew Bass was a man born to handle trouble. Besides she had reasons of her own for wanting Bass to take the job. He would be instrumental in cleaning up the Territory and making it a more fitting place to live. Jinney had never forgotten how her people had been driven from their peaceful homes. For her there was always the hope that she would someday return to the land of her birth, to her home in the Indian Territory. With Bass a part of the effort to clean up the Territory, she would be that much closer to going home. Though she hated violence and feared for her husband's safety, she put her trust in God and stood by Bass one hundred percent. With her blessing, Bass accepted the job.

CHAPTER **SIX**
Deputy Marshal Bass Reeves

The sun shone brightly in the sky. A crowd had gathered around the courthouse, mostly Black folk. Everyone had come to witness history in the making. Many marveled at the fact that in 1875 a Black man was going to be sworn in as a Deputy U. S. Marshal. "Was a time, many knew, when the thought of a Black man walking around carrying a gun, much less arresting people was unheard of." This day it would not only be heard of, it would be a reality.

Paralee walked through the crowd, her head held high, almost proud to busting. She tried hard not to outright grin, but it was a challenge. John Brady escorted his proud mother-in-law.

Jinney walked with Janie and the children. Murmurs rippled through the crowd as they passed, they were the 'Reeves' family. The Blacks and Indians admired them as did some of the Whites. However, the opinion of the White people in the crowd was mixed. Most thought Judge Parker had taken leave of his senses. The very idea of a Black man carrying a gun and having the authority to arrest a White man was hardly conceivable. They could not believe that Parker was actually going to swear in a Black Deputy Marshal, a deputy who would have the same rights and responsibilities as any other deputy. To some White citizens, that act in itself was a crime. Then there were White citizens who lived on the border of the Territory, they were thankful for any help in maintaining law and order. The color of a deputy's skin was not an issue for them, as long as he could keep their families and farms safe; that was all that really mattered to them. Whether or not they agreed with Judge Parker's belief that all citizens were equal before the law, was beside the point.

The Reeves family stopped at the door. The room was nearly filled to capacity with only standing room left. The pastor and members of Mt. Olive were already inside the courtroom. Many had arrived before day to claim their place. Recognizing the family, several kind souls stepped out to allow Paralee and her family into the room. No one seemed to notice the close quarters or that the air had difficulty circulating. Everyone's attention was drawn to the tall Black man standing in front of the room.

It wasn't hard to spot Bass, he stood a head taller than most. This day Bass wore his 'Sunday go to meeting' black suit. His shirt was bright white and so heavily starched that it could have held up the jacket by itself. Janie had made the shirt herself and Paralee had starched it. Bass' bushy handlebar moustache looked as if it, too, had been starched into attention. Of all the people in the room, Bass seemed to be the calmest. It was not that the momentous occasion was lost on him. He was just quietly thankful that old Reba's predictions were coming to pass. Many was the time in his life that he thought back on those words of hers. He turned and searched the crowd for his mother and Jinney. He caught his mother's eye; her smile seemed to light up the entire room. She nodded at him, he nodded back, they both knew just how far he had come. He turned his gaze to Jinney, who sat tall and straight next to his mother. Jinney stared steadily at Bass, then blinked her eyes once in greeting. Suddenly, inexplicably, Bass felt a lump in his throat. They had all come a far piece to this day, Paralee through slavery and Jinney through the horrors of war.

"Thank you, Lord," Bass whispered quietly. The bailiff entered the room.

"All rise," the Bailiff called, "The honorable Isaac C. Parker presiding." Those that sat stood, those that stood, stood taller as Judge Issac Parker took the bench.

Everyone in the room listened quietly as Parker spoke. He spoke of the importance of the lawman in an orderly society. Parker spoke not only to the man standing in front of him, but to *all* the citizens gathered that day. He intoned that the job of a lawman was a sacred trust, a high calling. Upon administering the oath, Judge Parker turned Bass Reeves from an ordinary citizen to one entrusted with the safety and well-being of all citizens. The duties of a lawman did not end at the end of a day. A lawman was required to uphold the law and maintain order at all times. However, the Judge warned, those sworn to uphold the law were never above the law. Any deputy violating the law would be punished to the full extent of the law with no exceptions. The citizens of Fort Smith were happy indeed to hear him repeat this mantra of his. After the corruption and rampant crime of the last administration, reassurance that Parker's court would be completely different was welcome.

Turning his attention directly to Bass, the Judge continued. "And Bass Reeves, you have a unique opportunity to show law abiding citizens and outlaws alike that a Black Deputy U.S. Marshal is the equal of any law enforcement officer."

Bass nodded solemnly, "Yes Sir."

Judge Parker stood and walked towards Bass, he held in his hand a shiny tin star. Pinning it on Bass' coat, Parker looked up at the new deputy and smiled. "Deputy Reeves." Parker shook Bass's hand. A collective sigh ran through the crowd, then someone started clapping, and embarrassed, but smiling, Bass acknowledged the applause.

When Paralee was able to get her son off to the side away from the crowd, she spoke quietly to him. "Keep your mind in the Good Book, look to it when you don't know which way to go." Paralee was also mindful of Reba's words that Bass would *'see danger,'* but knew that it was necessary to make things right in accordance with God's will. She wanted to make sure that her son understood the power he had just been given. She didn't want it to go to his head. Nor did she want him to ever use his badge for revenge.

"Yes'm. " Bass hugged his mother and assured her that he had memorized many of the Bible passages she had taught him. He still remembered his father's words. "There's man's law and there's God's law." It was now his job to uphold man's law, but he would always be true to God's law. Bass was ever mindful of the power of man's law, it had made him a slave and a fugitive from the law. Then declared him a free man and now he proudly served the law. As a newly-minted deputy marshal, Bass felt joy, pride and gratitude at being a representative of the U.S. government whose laws had transformed him from a slave to a free and responsible citizen. Hence, the law for him was much more than words, it was a tangible way to do good and the only real means to assure justice for all. Little did he know that many years ahead, his faith in man's law would be severely tested. However on this day, the future was bright and greatness lay ahead.

***

The morning after his swearing-in, Bass met with Judge Parker and Marshal James F. Fagan in the Judge's chambers. The meeting with Fagan and Parker was brief. The judge stated that Fagan would explain the details of the deputy marshal's job. As Bass and Fagan prepared to leave Parker's office, Parker reached for his well-worn leather-bound Bible. Bass noted the simple gesture; it reinforced his faith in the judge. Both he and Parker shared a powerful belief in the dignity of the law and the Biblical prediction that the wicked would be punished. Many years later in speaking of Judge Parker, Bass stated, "He was such a mighty powerful man then and did so much good according to what the Bible said do. And he sure knew him some Bible. Ya' know, he was named after the old prophet Isaac."

Once in his office, the marshal offered Bass a seat. Bass, along with the citizens of Fort Smith, liked and respected James Fagan. Fagan had been appointed marshal a year earlier. President Grant had ordered Fagan to clean up the corruption that had surrounded the marshal's office. A newspaper article demonstrated his popularity:

> *The relation this country bears to the United States government makes the marshal's office for the Western District of Arkansas of the most vital importance to us. In fact we are dependent solely upon it for the preservation of our lives and our property. But for this protection, no honest man could live in the Territory. The present incumbent, James F. Fagan, was raised on our border, and is well known to most of our people, and we will venture to say that nine-tenths would rather see him in the position than any man that could be appointed. Before he came into office we have been imposed upon to such an extent that our best citizens had come to look upon U.S. deputy marshals as*

a greater curse than the thieves and murderers that infested the country, and of the two evils they preferred taking their chances among the latter.[1]

Bass was also familiar with Fagan from his days working in the old court. Bass knew Fagan to be a fair and honest man. Deputy Marshal Reeves listened as Marshal Fagan outlined the duties and day-to-day activities of the deputies. For Bass it was merely a formality. He had worked around the court long enough to be familiar with the deputies' job. He knew what the pay scale was before he had accepted Parker's offer. Deputies were paid six cents a mile when on official business, fifty cents for serving papers, two dollars for each arrest, and one dollar for expenses. Seventy-five cents a day was allotted to feed each prisoner, however, the government did not pay for Bass' meals and the meals of any help that he hired. Deputies and their help were responsible for their own meals. Even though the possibility of injury and death on the job was extremely high, there was no compensation for deputies who were killed or crippled in the line of duty. Put in the context of money and benefits, it was not a very desirable job. Bass simply nodded his head, he was familiar with the routine. Fagan continued, reminding Bass that killing a wanted man brought on added expenses for the deputy. If family members or friends could not be located, then the deputy had to pay any burial expenses.

Fagan stopped and looked at Bass, "Don't nobody get rich as a deputy. Least wise if he's honest."

"I knows that." The pay was not the driving force for Bass. He had to finally admit to himself that he liked being out in the open, liked the chase, the challenge. Besides, he was damn good at it. He said as much to Fagan who laughed, "Ain't pressed for modesty, are ya, Bass?" Bass shook his head, "no."

The other factor that neither man mentioned was Judge Parker. Parker offered them a chance to bring real law and order to the frontier. Both men knew that hundreds of innocent people were being victimized by the outlaws. As Parker said at the swearing in, being a lawman was a calling, and they knew that the judge counted heavily on them. He often said, "Without these men, I could not hold court a single day. It takes men who are brave to uphold the law here."

Fagan went on with his briefing; he took out the expense records, file vouchers and a copy of an arrest warrant and handed them to Bass. "These likely all the papers you'll have to work with." Bass picked up the papers handed to him, looked at them briefly and then handed them back to Fagan.

"I can't cipher those. Can't read nor write."

It was the first big stumbling block in Bass' career. Deputies were required to keep records and read warrants, requirements that could have ended Bass' career before it began. Bass Reeves had learned a great deal in the intervening years since his escape from slavery, but he had never learned to read or write. At that moment in Fagan's office, Bass may have thought back on another day when he was a young man and he had asked Stewart for permission to learn to read. With a heavy sigh, both men sat staring at the papers that lay on the desk between them. Not a man to dwell on what could have been, Bass knew that a solution had to be found. He was a man used to finding answers to problems. He had escaped slavery, survived the Civil War and made a way for himself and his family. He would find a way around this obstacle as well.

Isaac Parker was also a man who saw an obstacle as a challenge. The U.S. Department of Justice had given Parker free rein in operating his court in any manner that he saw fit. Parker told Bass that he was not about to allow illiteracy to rob him of what he hoped would be one of his best deputies. In this instance, the sword was mightier than the pen. Parker assigned the court clerk to help Bass with all matters requiring reading and writing. The solution would work fine in the courthouse; but once in the

Territory the story would change. The clerk could not follow Bass while he went after outlaws.

Bass figured out a solution. He had the clerk read aloud writs (arrest warrants) issued by the judge, Bass memorized the name as it was spoken and written. It was an elementary form of reading, and perhaps Bass had a photographic memory.

In the field, to safeguard that he had the correct person, Bass insisted that a suspect read the warrant aloud to insure that he had indeed located the right person. There were however times when the person in question was also illiterate. In these instances, Bass relied on the help of his friends to make sure that he arrested the correct person. Like other circumstances in his life, the serving of warrants seemed also charmed. Deputy Marshal Bass Reeves served several thousand warrants during his career, in all that time, he never served the wrong person.

In addition to his extensive knowledge of the Territory, Bass was physically suited to his job. An erect, imposing, deep bronze figure standing well over six feet, he was more than 200 pounds of hardened muscle. His daughter, Alice, told of one incident that dramatized his strength and resourcefulness that occurred while he was riding in the southern part of the Chickasaw Nation. Bass came upon cowboys struggling to free a large steer deeply mired in a muddy bog. The cowboys had tugged with ropes and horses nearly two hours and were about to give up. After watching a few minutes, Bass dismounted, removed his guns and most of his clothes, then approached the trapped animal. Disengaging the ropes, which had practically strangled the steer, he quietly talked to it while moving about, pushing, pulling and lifting the animal by its horns. Slowly dislodging it from the bog's suction, he repeated the process until the steer lunged forward to solid footing and freedom. Then Bass exited the bog, wiped off the mud and rode off toward the nearest clear creek without ever speaking a word to the awestruck cowboys.

Having the proper tools of the trade posed no problem for Bass since guns and trusty mounts had long been part of his life. He also was never without the assistance of a highly trained dog. Although Judge Parker had issued an order on a local hardware store for the purchase of the necessary weapons, Bass owned several fine guns. However, he purchased a heavy caliber longgun and a small caliber pistol to carry in his boot. On the trail, he kept most of his weapons in a small trunk on the grub wagon. Usually, he rode with a Winchester rifle and wore either two Colt 45's or a single .44 pistol on his right side. In addition to the heavy caliber rifle, a double-barreled shotgun was always available.

Although declaring his performance with a rifle only fair, Bass allegedly could shoot the hind leg off a fly sitting on a mule's ear and never disturb the mule. Because of his skill, he was barred from turkey shoots and competitions at fairs and picnics. Alice remembered a story her father told about his prowess with a gun. On one occasion while riding in a remote area, Bass came over a hill just as six wolves began attacking a steer. While moving on horseback, he killed all six with eight shots. He broke one wolf's leg and "gut shot" the other the first time around. Although he stopped both animals with the first shot, he used a second shot to end their suffering.

Bass' knowledge of handguns was limited until he met Arch Landon while working for the railroad. Landon taught him that the key to handling a gun was to quickly get it into action and fire it accurately. Hardly a day passed that Bass did not practice drawing and shooting. He never forgot Landon's advice for using his gun in close quarters. He should hit his opponent with the barrel of his gun, never the butt, to avoid accidental firing. If the encounter came to a shoot-out, Bass' friend stressed the importance of making the first shot count, since "the man must go down and stay down or he will surely kill you." Landon insisted that a good lawman in the territory must be prepared to kill.

Since his early years, Bass had been extremely fond of horses and reputedly could "do horse talk." Traveling across the open land, whether along trails or back country, he constantly chattered with both his horse and dog as if they were part of each other. Even at night, they slept close together so that he could be quickly alerted to any unseen danger. Because of 200-pounds, Bass preferred a "big, well-bodied horse," a sorrel or bay. "When you get as big as me," he explained, "a small horse is as worthless as a preacher in a whiskey joint fight. Just when you need him to help you out, he's got to stop and think about it a little bit."

The speed of a horse had its advantages, but of primary concern to Bass was its strength and endurance. Being certain of where he was going was more important than how fast he got there.

Alice told of a story that demonstrated the wisdom of her father's choice of horse. She learned from Allen Thompson, a former cowboy, about a horse race in which he and Bass had put each other's favorite mount to the test.

The two men chanced to meet along the upper reaches of Hell Roaring Creek in the Chickasaw Nation. Bass was on his way to the Creek Nation, carrying a pocketful of writs. He rode a big sorrel gelding, almost a full 19 hands tall. Thompson was working the brush along the creek for stray cattle, and he rode a little gray mare, hardly bigger than a "Spanish mule."

The two decided to race even though each claimed his horse was slow, hard-working, untrained, and generally incapable of sustained competition. The course was set at two miles, and each bet $20 to help the winner reconcile the strain and effort that his 'po' old wore-out horse', would have to exert. Bass tossed a rock over his shoulder into the creek. Its splashing sound was their signal to move out. With perhaps not another living soul closer than 40 miles, Bass and Thompson raced down the fertile bottom land of Hellroaring Creek.

Thompson's little gray mare was off like a guinea hen in a hail storm. Bass later learned that it was one of the top horses in the Chickasaw Nation, and Thompson had beaten all comers in matched races. Predictably, Bass' sorrel, at the start, was left sittin' and wonderin'. Suddenly, Bass yelled in a hoarse tone, shifted his weight forward in the saddle, and the big gelding accelerated.

Despite its weight, Bass' horse was graceful and fast, and his long, powerful strides soon had the sorrel closing in on the gray. By the three-quarter mark, the gray no longer had a chance. As the sorrel passed the gray, Thompson grunted in disbelief. He had urged his horse along, even used his whip, but the sorrel was too far ahead. Sitting back, he pulled up the gray and allowed her to finish the race in an easy gait. He would not break her heart by letting her finish a race in which she was so greatly overmatched. Thompson later complained, "That damned sorrel cost me my last twenty bucks."

Aside from Fagan, there were other members of Parker's court that Bass was familiar with. Many were men that he had interacted with in the past. However, this time he was on an indisputable equal level with them. For some it might have been a problem, for Bass it was his due.

The more notable of the men in Parker's court were prosecutor U.S. Attorney William H. H. Clayton (a former judge) and George Winston who was Parker's bailiff. Winston was a Black man and former army veteran who had also served in the Storey court. Special Deputy Marshal George Maledon was a former Fort Smith policeman and deputy sheriff. Maledon was appointed special deputy marshal in charge of execution of condemned prisoners. During the 22 years of serving the Parker's court, he performed the execution of 60 criminals—more than any other man in modern times. His cool efficiency and dedication gained him the title "Prince of Hangmen."

Bass remembered the stories Arch Landon, the former deputy from his railroad days, had told him. According to Arch, the hostile atmosphere they had faced with the railroad workers was nothing compared to the dangers faced by deputy marshals in the Territory. Landon had often told him that being a deputy in the Indian Territory was the most dangerous job of any man who wore a badge. Unlike the railroad, the Territory was not a controlled environment. Deputies often worked alone and ambush was a constant threat. In order to stay alive, a deputy had to be quick with a gun and able to out think the outlaws.

Bass was confident that he had the skills to do both. From his own experience, he knew that trailing outlaws was extremely risky with odds favoring the criminals. Holed up in the mountains or along densely wooded river bottoms, outlaws had a natural sanctuary from which they could ambush lawmen.

Many outlaws, once found, preferred to resist arrest, rather than be brought in to face Judge Parker. Word had spread that anyone convicted of a hanging offense was as good as hung. Bass knew that he had to be prepared for anything, and he felt that he was. It would seem that his entire life thus far had prepared him for the job of deputy marshal. He brought with him all that he had learned living with the various Indians in the Territory. The lessons he had learned from the Lighthorse would prove to be invaluable. As he thought about it, Bass could not help but believe that he had been destined to become a lawman. He hoped that Old Reba could see him now.

With a bushy moustache, he was deceptively stern-faced with a smile that came easily but not often. His rich brown eyes reflected the contradictions within him. They were direct and piercing, yet soft and all-encompassing. His voice was deep and resonant with a decidedly commanding tone. His proud carriage and bearing marked one who believed there was hardly anything he could not handle. Bass was not quarrelsome or easily disturbed, but was quick to take a sharp issue with anyone who spoke disparagingly about his character or color. To make his point, he was prepared to use his fists or even his guns if necessary.

CHAPTER **SEVEN**
Enforcing the Law

Bass' official duties commenced with a brief stint working around the court, mainly guarding defendants and searching spectators for weapons. Many times Bass watched the people who were watching the proceedings. All banter ceased after the defendants were brought in because Parker was close behind. Spectators sat as "obedient school children" for Parker was known to levy heavy fines for any outbursts or unruly conduct in his courtroom.

Deputy Marshal Reeves' first field assignment was enforcing liquor laws. Assignments began when Judge Parker signed a warrant directing that criminal offenders be brought in dead or alive. However, arrest warrants were not needed if offenders were caught in the act. Though Parker did insist that all of his deputies follow procedures when making an arrest, if a deputy did not have a writ in hand for a suspect, they were required to send for one. Many deputies failed to comply, thereby creating great hardship for the court and the parties. Bass, however, scrupulously followed the rules, which was the key to securing convictions and insuring his personal risks were not in vain. Court records show that whenever possible, he not only requested the issuance of writs (arrests warrants), but he also provided names of witnesses[1] on January 30, 1883, he wrote Marshal boles from the Seminole nation:

> *I have captured a Seminole for selling whiskey Saturday night January 27th. He had 2 1/2 gallons. His name is Sammy Lowe. Please issue a writ and forward to me at McAllister.*
>
> *The witnesses are Parmaskah and Jim Kindar. I have also captured Cantille the man that escaped from Mershon.*
> *Please hold the writ.*
>
> *I am getting along very well and will be in about the 13th Feb.*

From Okmullkee on October 6, 1885, he wrote the Marshal:

> *Send me writs for the following persons. Send toSansakawa Seminole Nation. I caught them in the act of selling myself.*

Amos Gray. Introducing and selling 3 gal. Whiskey Sunday Oct. 4, 1885.

William Anderson. Introducing and selling 2 1/2 gal. Whiskey Oct. 4, 1885.

I am doing well. I have all under arrest. I will start for Sansakawa tomorrow.

Later, on December 26, 1889, he wrote from Wewaka after arresting one TaTutsie for introducing spirituous liquors, that:

He introduced 2 gals. Whiskey. I caught him with same.

Lee Jefferson will swear that this Indian had 2 gals. Whiskey and tasted of it and will swear that it was whiskey.

I will swear to catching him with the whiskey, and also tasted it and will swear it was whiskey.

The correspondence was obviously written by those in the small towns who were anxious to assist Bass.

Judge Parker believed that drinking was the curse of the frontier. In his opinion, more than half the crimes committed west of Arkansas were due to whiskey. Cracking down on the illegal traffic of liquor was the main part of his plan to clean up the Territory. Though the sale of whiskey and other alcoholic drinks was legal in Fort Smith, it was illegal in the Territory. However, whether in the Territory or Fort Smith, it was illegal to sell, barter, or give whiskey to Indians. Operating a distillery to produce whiskey bound for Indians or Indian Territory also violated federal laws. Regardless, liquor flowed freely.

Heading into the Territory on long trips, Bass usually left Fort Smith with a wagon, a cook, and a posse-man or guard. Posse-men were registered with the marshal's office. Guards were hired only to guard prisoners and drive the wagons; they were under no obligation to provide any other help. In some cases he would leave without a guard, but decide once out on the trail to hire one. For the most part, Bass began his assignments with a posse-man. He usually had a well-thought-out plan for capturing his prisoners. Sometimes he would leave his wagon and posse-man camped in a central location. Other times he would arrange to meet at a certain point while he went in search of wanted outlaws.

Bass began his career by using his skin color to his advantage when possible. So many others had used it to their advantage and his disadvantage; it was time the tables were turned. From conversations with Bass, his daughter Alice firmly believed that concealing his identity might have meant the difference between life and death on many occasions. Most people, Black, Red or White never expected a Black man to be a Deputy Marshal. From his previous experience with the bounty hunters and deputies, Bass knew that to most he was invisible. Folks had a tendency to discount Black people. Most times White folk never thought of a Black person as a full, intelligent human being. Bass used this to his advantage by disguising himself as a cowboy, drifter or outlaw seeking a drink. He made numerous arrests because most whiskey peddlers simply did not expect a Black man to be a federal officer. In addition to the ability to disguise himself, Bass had another asset that he used to track down and arrest criminals, his friendships with a number of Indians in the Territory.

Bass' friends were willing to help him, especially in the pursuit of those selling whiskey in their communities. Bootleg whiskey was a serious threat to the health and well-being of their people. Bootleg whiskey was not regulated, often the whiskey sold in the Territory was poisonous, causing serious illness, blindness and even death. White marshals could not get the cooperation or help that Bass got. Though they feared reprisals, most Indians were eager to help Bass eliminate alcohol in the Territory. They passed valuable information along to Bass, especially the locations of various stills and the general whereabouts of whiskey peddlers. To avoid endangering his friends, Bass usually traveled alone in search of stills often hidden under clusters of vines and shrubs. Arriving in an area where he believed a still was located, he relied on a low growl from his dog or the flicking of his horse's ears to signal the hidden activity. Bass' first shoot-out occurred while trying to arrest a whiskey peddler.

Bass was working with two Indian friends when he spotted a known whiskey peddler's wagon. Bass told his friends to follow the wagon and ask for a drink. While his friends rode towards the wagon, Bass left the road and circled around to position himself in front. Taking cover among the brush he waited. Pretending to be drunk, the Indians told the peddler they wanted to buy more whiskey. Eager to conduct business, the peddler had the driver halt the wagon. He stepped down from the wagon. Bass watched the scene play just as he had planned. He looked at the wagon driver and the hairs prickled on the back of his neck. The man seated next to the driver had not moved, a shotgun lay across his lap aimed in the direction of the Indians, this man was a hired gunman. Bass looked quickly at his friends, one of them had purchased a bottle of whiskey and was haggling over a cheaper price for the second. The peddler, intent on selling the second bottle at the same price, did not at first notice the Black man who appeared on the opposite side of the wagon, gun drawn. "U.S. Marshal, drop them guns and raise your hands!" The peddler immediately raised his hands, but the gunman began cursing. "A Black badge don't mean a damned thing to me!" He swung the rifle towards Bass; in mid-swing, Bass fired two bullets into his chest. He was dead before he fell from the driver's seat. Bass never forgot that first killing. He also never forgot that Arch Landon's advice had served him well. "Make the first shot count."

The danger in pursuing illegal traffickers was a continuing problem. Marshal Carrol warned his deputies:

> *Don't ever underestimate a whiskey peddler. It is a felony to sell whiskey to the Indians, and it is not the kind of a charge that most men would be willing to get into a shoot-out over. They come along peacefully enough once you catch them. But there is always that exception that a lawman must watch for at all times—if he intends to stay alive.*

The marshal's concern was legitimate, because in just one year, Carrol had lost five deputies and four posse-men who were murdered in the line of duty.[2] Bass figured that to stay alive he must gain an edge on his adversary whenever possible. He thus became quite adept at passing himself off as someone other than a lawman.

Bass was able to arrest a fair amount of whiskey peddlers, but it became obvious to Parker that sporadic arrests of whiskey peddlers were not making a dent in the whiskey trade in the Territory; a different approach was needed. Parker wanted his deputies to go after only those who made a business of introducing whiskey to Indians. Most arrests were of lesser offenders, while the major liquor traffickers went free. It was also impossible to secure warrants to search all of the freight wagons legitimately in the Territory although liquor was usually stored in the wagon beds under other goods.

Just as legal freight was distributed from Fort Smith, Bass was convinced that illegal liquor was also distributed in the same manner. Bass decided he would cut off the flow of the illegal liquor traffic at its source, if possible, rather than attempting to block all the outlets.

Bass was convinced that most of the whiskey in the Territory came from the same source as the legal freight that was distributed from Fort Smith. He figured that the whiskey was simply not ferried across the Arkansas River to the Territory with other freight. The whiskey was probably sent across the river from hidden landing sites. Bass again teamed with old friends and other Indians to scout the river for possible landing sites. Their work paid off, a spot was located north of Fort Smith where a number of farm wagon tracks converged at the river. The area, dense with undergrowth, had a small loading dock. Although some of the tracks were reasonably fresh, there was no sign of continuous activity.

Once they identified a landing site, Bass set about determining where the whiskey could be stored. Subtle investigation around town revealed that whiskey was stored in a warehouse that did not ordinarily distribute liquor to any of the local businesses. Bass also learned that freight wagons were periodically loaded at this particular warehouse in the evening then left at night for parts unknown. This information fit in with his theory that the liquor was moved under cover of night. This was evidence he needed. Bass put his plan in motion. Several of his friends would follow the wagon. But that night the wagon did not travel toward the river. Instead, it moved east apparently destined for legal trade east of Fort Smith. Disappointed, Bass' friends decided to follow the wagon anyway, just in case. It was a wise choice. On the outskirts of Fort Smith, the wagon abruptly left the road. The scouts followed the wagon as it swung north onto a seldom-used trail. They reported back to Bass.

The next day, Bass followed the same road out of Fort Smith to the trail his scouts had told him about. The trail eventually circled back to the river. There, two barges were waiting.

This was the landing site they had been looking for! Because of a bend in the river, it ceased to be the boundary with the Territory.

A week went by with no activity at the river nor the warehouse. Bass and his friends kept watch on both places. Several days later, he received word that the wagons were again being loaded at the warehouse. Bass had calculated where the barges were likely to land on the other side. He crossed the river at Fort Smith as arranged with the Indian Lighthorse. Bass then rode toward the point on the river where the barges were expected, found a good hiding place and waited. As he waited, several farm wagons arrived at the riverbank. Bass had to move farther away from his hiding place to avoid being caught. The barges drew up to the bank. Bass kept his distance and watched as the wagons were loaded with liquor. He waited until the wagons crossed the border into Indian Territory. Stepping out of the woods, he halted the wagons and this time made his arrests without bloodshed. Bass confiscated the liquor, wagons and horses as well.

***

The Fort Smith jail was filled with prisoners that first year. Parker's court was in session almost continuously. During the summer, he sentenced six murderers to die on the gallows. The executions were set for early September. Parker was determined to demonstrate that swift and sure punishment awaited anyone convicted of crimes within his jurisdiction. On the morning of September 23, 1875, six men prepared to meet their death. Bass was familiar with each of the condemned men and their crimes. The following men were brought out into the light of day for the last time:

1). John Whittington who clubbed his neighbor and slashed his throat after spending the day drinking with him. His motive, money.

2). Dan Evans riddled his friend's body with bullets for a pair of boots and a saddle.
3). James Moore, a horse thief, killed a deputy while resisting arrest.
4). Smoker Mankiller borrowed his neighbor's rifle then calmly killed him. The motive was never clear.
5). Edmund Campbell settled a dispute with his friend by killing him and his daughter after a prayer service.
6). Sam Fooy, a known gambler and thief, bashed in the head of John Neff, a school teacher, for his $250 end-of-his-school term pay.

In contrasting the lifestyles of Fooy and Neff, Bass could clearly see the urgency of his mission. One lived in total defiance of the law and an orderly society, posing an ever-present threat to all that was decent in the land. The other was singularly dedicated to helping the younger generation prepare for a brighter future in the same land that so sorely needed respect and protection of the law.

A crowd gathered outside of the jail. Several thousand persons from all walks of life, within a 50 to 60 mile radius, had traveled to Fort Smith during the week before to observe the spectacle. This event would earn Judge Parker the nickname "The Hanging Judge." It was to follow him the rest of his life.

Inside the jail, the foot shackles were removed promptly at 10:00 a.m. The convicted men marched nearly 100 yards across the jail yard to the base of the gallows. The procession was led by four clergymen and heavily armed guards who walked to the side and rear of the 10-foot-high platform. The width of the gallows ran about 20 feet long with two planks, each about two feet wide, hinged and opening together like table leaves. Single file, the condemned men walked the 12 steps to the platform where each was directed to stand under a dangling rope attached to a sturdy overhead beam. Deputy Maledon instructed the prisoners to line their feet up across the line where the hinged planks formed the death trap. After prayers, hymns and last farewells, a black cap was placed over the head of each condemned man and the nooses adjusted. Maledon, who had prepared the ropes well and tested the mechanism, pulled the lever that released the trigger bar.

Newspaper accounts across the nation expressed shock at the event, referring to it in one headline as the "Cool Destruction of Six Human Lives by Legal Process." Persons unfamiliar with the godless Territory might have believed that "None but a heartless judge could be so lacking in compassion as to decree such wholesale killing." However, J. W. Weaver, a reporter for the *Western Independent* and correspondent of the *New York Herald*, wrote:

> *They are preying wolves upon the lives and property of their fellow beings, unfit to live and unsafe to remain at large. He noted that, "Society, through the stern mandates of the law, has thus consigned them to death and exterminated them from the face of the earth.*[3]

Reactions to the hangings were the first national criticism of the Parker court. The judge's response was "If criticism is due, it should be the system, not the man whose duty lies under it." Though Parker became known as, "Hanging Judge Parker," ironically, he was against capital punishment. He often said, "I have never hanged a man. It is the law." He further explained, "I favor its [hanging's] abolition, provided there is certainty of punishment. It is certainty of punishment that halts crime."

Bass understood the Judge's stance. Though killing was never something he enjoyed, he knew that in many instances in order to survive, to fulfill his duty, it was kill or be killed.

CHAPTER **EIGHT**
The Ties That Bind

The Reeves family settled into a routine. Paralee spent much of her time at Mt. Olive with various church activities. Jinney and Janie were kept busy with chores and Janie's growing brood. John ran the farm in Bass' absence.

Although Jinney's days were filled with chores, baby sitting and lending a hand at the school when needed, her nights were probably the hardest. This was the time when she missed her husband the most. She wondered where he was and if he was safe. Life as the wife of a deputy marshal was harder than she had first thought. She knew that there were people who wanted nothing better than to kill her husband. She knew this for a fact because Bass had brought home notes left for him along the trail, and asked her to read them to him. They were from one desperado or another, warning Bass, that if he kept after them, they would kill him. The notes didn't seem to bother Bass. He'd just nod and put them in a box. Sometimes he'd even laugh, especially when he had already arrested the author of the note! Jinney always looked forward to Bass' return. Typically a trip lasted no more than thirty days. Usually each trip resulted in no less than four hundred dollars in pay. For Jinney, the money took a back seat to the fact that Bass had returned safely.

Jinney especially looked forward to Bass' return this trip. There was a new baby in the family. Even though the child was not theirs, Jinney had been smitten with little William Brady (destined to become the author's father). He was so inquisitive, even at his tender age. She knew that Bass liked babies though he pretended not to. She wanted to see him with little William, she could pretend for a little while that he was theirs. With the birth of William, Jinney redoubled her prayers for a baby of her own.

***

Bass rode his big sorrel into camp. A group of deputies had converged at the site. When Bass joined them at the fire, they were talking about the five thousand dollar reward offered. Had Bass heard about it? Bass sat and helped himself to a cup of coffee, "Can't say as I have." Eager to tell the story, the deputy explained that two fugitive brothers were on the run. Five thousand dollars had been offered for their capture. The brothers were wanted for a variety of crimes. They had proven impossible to catch. Bass interrupted him, "I'll catch em." The other deputies laughed. Bass said nothing else, just sat back and listened.

Bass left the camp determined to find the wanted brothers. Everywhere he went he sought information from his Indian friends in the area, asking questions and talking with people along the way. Typically prison wagons covered a great deal of land, tracking one outlaw then another. Prison wagons were dubbed tumbleweed wagons, after the broken-off tumbleweeds rolling across the flat countryside, stopping, then rolling again, first in one direction then another. This seemingly aimless wandering proved a good way to gain information. Travelers would often change course when they saw a prison wagon, curious to find out who had been captured. Bass welcomed the opportunity to talk with the travelers and exchange news. Any information could prove valuable.

Soon Bass had pieced together a pattern that the brothers followed, their modus operandi was to hole up at their mother's cabin in a remote wooded area near the Texas border. Upon further investigation, Bass learned the general whereabouts of the cabin. This, he figured was the best place to catch the outlaws. He would let them come to him. But how was he going to get to the house and wait for the outlaws without drawing attention to himself? What disguise and reason could he use to get close enough to the house? After some thought Bass had a plan.

He took his wagon, the prisoners that he had already captured, and a man named Campbell who acted as cook and guard and headed towards the border. The prisoners were understandably surly and intent on escaping rather than appearing in Parker's court. No matter how capable with fists or guns, a careless guard could be overwhelmed by the sheer number of prisoners in his wagon or by the prisoners' relatives attempting ambushes along the trail to court.

By now the prisoners knew that Bass was after the notorious brothers and the five thousand dollar reward. Several prisoners taunted him that he would never see the green of that money. No one had captured the brothers and Bass wouldn't either. Deputy Bass rode on in silence, not bothering to respond to the taunts. He stopped about twenty miles from the border and made camp.

It was Bass' custom to collect a number of prisoners before heading back to Fort Smith. It just made good money sense to him. Adding the two brothers to this batch of prisoners would more than make this trip an all time high. Besides, he loved a challenge.

Once he brought in 16 prisoners, collecting $700 in fees while his expenses came to less than $100. His biggest haul was believed to be 17 prisoners which brought him about $900. The fee system ended in 1898 when salaries ranged from $500 to $2,500 a year. In addition, rewards were often received from private individuals, local and state authorities, and railroads.

With Campbell's help, Bass hauled a long log out of the wagon and let it drop to the ground. They rolled the log beside the wagon and placed it flat side up; Campbell then marched the prisoners to the log and had them sit. The log had been especially cut for this purpose. Bass and Campbell placed leg irons on each prisoner, shackled them together, then drove a pin into the ground, securing them for the day. At night the chain would be wrapped around the wagon axle and locked. After securing the prisoners, Bass began his preparations.

Pulling out a pair of shabby pants and a shirt from his bundle, he changed. The clothes looked like they had been patched together with a cactus needle. The ragged clothes were purposefully shapeless and big enough to hide handcuffs and six shooters. Amused, Campbell watched Bass transform himself. On the way to the border, Bass had stopped shaving, adding to his disguise; this time Bass was a hapless drifter. Next, he took out a pair of old boots and proceeded to knock the heels off with the handle of his gun. To complete the disguise, Bass pulled out an old beat-up hat and shot holes in it. Campbell could not help but laugh when Bass plopped the hat on his head. Grinning, Bass asked, "Don't look like no marshal, do I?" Unable to stop laughing, Campbell could only shake his head no. Bass sat down to clean and prepare his guns for the next morning.

Early the next day, Bass started out from his camp on foot. The cabin was several miles away. By walking to the mother's cabin, Bass figured that he wouldn't arouse suspicion. By the time Bass arrived at the cabin, he was dusty, dirty, and in real need of food and water. His lips were dry and slightly cracked, dust and grit had settled into his moustache turning it from black to a brownish gray.

An older woman stood outside the cabin and watched his approach. Hands on hips, she asked him to state his business. Bass noticed that there was a shotgun behind her within easy reach. He stopped several yards from the woman and took his hat off his head. "Ma'am," he said, his voice cracked and hoarse, "I ain't had no food or water in a mighty while. If'n you be a mind I trade ya some grub for chores?" The woman studied Bass carefully, she could use some help and he was a sorry sight indeed. Bass remained where he had stopped and waited patiently. He licked his parched lips and tried to wipe some of the dirt out of the corners of his eyes. For good measure, he swayed just a tad.

Satisfied that he posed no threat, especially in his seemingly weak condition, the woman invited him into the sod cabin. Bass nodded his appreciation and asked if he might wash himself up a bit before he entered her house. She shrugged and directed him to the side of the house where the well sat. As Bass drank thirstily from the dipping spoon on the bucket, he surveyed the lay of the land. There was a barn in the back of the house, an old chicken coop to the side, and a chopping block in front of the barn. Pouring water on his hands to clean them, then on his face, Bass wiped both with the sleeve of his shirt. All the while he felt the woman's eyes on him. She was a cautious one he thought. But then that was to be expected. Bass turned and headed towards the cabin.

As Bass sopped up stew with a hunk of dry cornbread, he told his tale of woe. His story was that he had been chased by lawmen. He told of barely escaping with his life. His poor horse had been shot out from under him, causing him to scramble and hide in the woods. Piteously, he showed the three holes in his hat. Shaking his head sadly he commented on how lucky he was that the same bullets hadn't put three similar holes in his old head. Sympathizing, the mother told him that the law was also hounding her boys. For a time she and Bass cursed the very ground that lawmen walked on, then the mother told Bass that maybe he could join up with her boys and they could work together. Bass nodded in agreement, he'd like that. He told the old woman that it was hard being just one man trying to keep clear of the damn lawmen.

After his meal, Bass went out back to chop wood as he had promised. He didn't chop a lot because he knew that he would need his strength when the sons arrived, plus, he didn't want to seem too strong. As long as he was thought of as a weak man, he would pose no threat.

With the wood pilled neatly by the door, Bass went inside and sat beside the fire with the mother. He pretended to doze, exhausted from the chopping. A little after nightfall, Bass heard a sharp whistle from the woods. The mother immediately jumped up and hurried outside. She answered with a whistle of her own. Bass stirred himself, but did not move from his spot by the fire. Soon he heard two horses ride up to the cabin. He could hear the mother explaining his presence. Her sons were not happy to hear that a stranger was in the cabin. The three argued for a time then the mother finally convinced them that Bass was not only harmless, he was a potential ally. Reluctantly, they put their horses in the barn and entered the cabin. Bass sat where she had left him. He had his hat in his hands. He was introduced to the sons who eyed him suspiciously.

As they sat at the table eating, Bass again told his tale of escape from the law. By the time the brothers had finished their meal, they had relaxed, believing Bass' story. Though they were not entirely comfortable with him, he was directed to sleep in the barn. This was not what Bass wanted to do, it would make the arrests more difficult. Instead, he suggested that they all sleep in one room. Full of suspicion, the oldest brother wanted to know why they should do that. Bass explained that he had the law after him, and they had the law after them. So, it was likely that they could get ambushed in the middle of the night by a number of lawmen. Wouldn't it be safer if they were all in the same place? They'd have a better chance of taking down anybody who came after them. Bass' argument did make sense. All four decided to bed down in the same room for the night. Bass stayed up awhile talking with the brothers, then he feigned sleep and pretended to drift off mid-sentence. After several hours, the cabin was quiet, and everyone was asleep, everyone but the deputy. Stealthily, Bass removed the handcuffs hidden under his clothes. He carefully slid guns from their holsters and moved them away from the sleeping brothers. Gently he handcuffed each brother. Bass stood towering above the sleeping outlaws, pulled the six shooter out of his belt with one hand, pulled out the writs with the other, and woke up the house with a deep strong voice that he had not used until now. "Wake up! This here be Deputy Marshal Bass Reeves, and I got writs for your arrest!" The confused brothers woke with a start to discover that they were handcuffed. Cursing, the mother went for her gun, only to find it empty. All three cursed Bass as he rousted the boys to their feet. "Come on boys, we gon' get going from here."[1] The mother of the boys followed Bass and his two prisoners for several miles, cursing Bass and calling him everything but a son of God. Finally, exhausted and defeated she gave up. Bass continued on to camp.

Back in camp, Bass shackled the brothers and added them to the heavy chain along with the other prisoners. Snapping the locks closed, he said, "Maybe now boys you know my money'll turn green."

That evening, as was his habit, Bass preached to the prisoners. He felt the need to talk to them of salvation, of right and wrong according to the Bible. He didn't like thinking that all he did was send men to prison, and in some cases to the gallows. Bass firmly believed that all criminal acts were the result of a lack of faith in God. His favorite quote was from First Psalms, "Blessed is the man that walketh not in the counsel of the ungodly but his delight is in the law of the Lord."

***

When Bass returned home, his nephew Johnny ran to greet him on the road to the house. Johnny was eager to tell Uncle Bass about his new brother, William, and hear how Uncle Bass had captured the bad guys.

Jinney had been right about the baby. There was something that seemed to pass between the large man with the giant hands and the tiny baby boy that held onto his finger. "Hello, little'un," Bass said. He was glad to be home, glad to see his wife and pleased that another Reeves had been born free. Bass gently removed his finger from the baby's grasp. He was weary and wanted a hot bath and some clean clothes. Jinney had sent someone to heat the bath water for him. He couldn't wait to settle down to hear the news on the ranch and catch up with the family. It was good to be home.

***

By the time Alice Reeves was born, her father had been a lawman for five years. He had earned the reputation of a deputy who was feared, hated and admired. Seemed like Bass Reeves more times than not got his man. Jinney and Bass were thrilled with the arrival of Alice. At long last their prayers had been answered. Jinney took great pride in her daughter, determined that she would have the best that her parents could offer. With Alice's arrival, Bass looked forward to his return home with greater anticipation. It always surprised him to see how much his daughter had grown in his absence. He marveled at her tiny hands and her questioning eyes. Bass had also grown extremely fond of little William Brady.

Years later William told his children many stories about his early years. It was generally known around the farm when Bass was expected home after trips. Eagerly the children gathered to greet him as he rode in tall and erect atop a large beautiful horse. He recalled that Bass was usually dressed in black or shades of brown, from his medium crowned hat with the wide brim to his polished boots. Uncle Bass always wore a clean white shirt. Pinned on his leather vest was his shiny badge, and on each side of his waist, guns. Fascinated with guns, William tried to be present whenever the guns were being taken off or put on. When Bass was dressed up, he always wore his guns high on the waist with the butts forward and protruding from his coat, a clear signal that Bass Reeves was ready for anything. William became attached to Bass during his stays in Van Buren. They spent a considerable time together hunting and fishing. William learned much about the outdoors from his Uncle Bass, who nicknamed him "Luck" for his ability to shoot game and catch fish when others could not. Another favorite pastime of Bass was listening to my father and Granny Paralee sing. Both had outstanding voices.

Part of Luck's earliest recollection of Uncle Bass was his hearty laughter and his playfulness. Not only did he entertain the youngsters, but he also enjoyed teasing his mother (Paralee) who seemed pleased that, at least for the immediate present, he was out of danger. Bass' time at home was spent catching up with the business of the farm, reacquainting himself with his wife and daughter, and fishing with Janie's boys. Always there was the big furry dog that the children were forbidden to touch except when Uncle Bass was present.

The impact of an officer of the law on the young boys in the family was profound. Sometimes little Luck could be seen attempting a Bass-like walk, which only served to earn him much good-natured teasing from his older brother and the other boys in the compound. Luck's older brother, Johnny, would eventually work in the Territory with Bass, as would Luck. However, before he was ready, Luck, too, would attempt to "ride" with Bass.

Overwhelmed by the stories told by his older brother, Luck secretly trailed Bass after he left the farm. When discovered several miles from home, Luck was severely scolded, and contrary to his expectations, was dispatched back to the house. Fortunately for Luck, only the horse was whipped, sending the disappointed boy home at a gallop.

The Reeves' settlement was home to several children who were not blood kin. Jinney had a habit of taking abandoned children under her wing. They were given chores to do, a roof over their heads, clean clothes and meals. But most of all, they were given love. In the evenings at home, Bass and Jinney would sit together on the porch and survey the home that they had created. They were both satisfied and proud that they had accomplished so much. They had much to be thankful for. Neither missed the opportunity to especially thank God for the good life that they led. Every Sunday that Bass was home, he attended church. He was a deacon at Mt. Olive and a much respected member of the community. Bass made a point not to wear his guns into town on Sunday. It was the Lord's day and he was mindful of it. In church Bass prayed for the chance to return to Mt. Olive and worship again, his next assignment on his mind.

***

Deputies Bass Reeves, Addison Beck, and George Maledon (the Prince of Hangmen) had been selected by Marshal Valentine Dell to accompany 21 prisoners to the

Federal House of Corrections in Detroit Michigan. It would be a long trip and with that many prisoners, there was a good possibility for a lot of trouble. To complicate matters even further, one of the prisoners was a woman with two children, a six-year-old and an infant that she had given birth to in the Fort Smith jail. Truth be told, Bass was not looking forward to this assignment. He much preferred being out in the Territory tracking and outwitting the outlaws. He was glad Addison was going, they were friends and they could count on each other to watch their backs.

They made the trip to Detroit by railroad. Changing trains in St. Louis, Bass and the other deputies herded the prisoners into the waiting room. The group attracted a lot of attention, especially the Black man ordering around White people, and most pointedly a White woman. The scene was apparently too much for one irate man, who barged his way into the midst of the prisoners shouting his objections to a Negro with a gun ordering White citizens around. One of the deputies working with Bass thought that the man was trying to break the prisoners free. The deputy sprang in front of the man, gun drawn. Ordering the man to remove himself from the prisoners, the deputy pointed the gun directly into the irate citizen's face. A local policeman rushed between the men, grabbing the marshal's revolver. Instantly all the deputies had their guns pointed at the policeman. Astonished, the police officer stood paralyzed. Just before the situation escalated into a blood bath, Marshal Dell walked in, and quickly assessed the state of affairs, and ordered his men to lay down their weapons (which they did). Dell explained to the policeman and the irate man that his men were U.S. Deputy Marshals transporting prisoners to the Federal House of Corrections in Detroit, and that Bass Reeves was also a U.S. Deputy Marshal. The trip to Detroit was made without further trouble. Two local Fort Smith newspapers chronicled the incident.[2]

The Detroit trip served to underscore the fact that the possibility of death in the line of duty was constant. Many lawmen were not as lucky as Bass and Addison were that day. Bass knew many of the 103 lawmen, who, not as fortunate as he, were killed in the performance of their duties. Sadly, two years after the Detroit trip, Addison Beck became one of the officers killed in the line of duty. Bass and several of Addison's friends responded quickly in seeking the capture of the killers.

***

Ironically, Bass had sporadic friendships with some of the Territory's most infamous outlaws. Noteworthy was his closeness to the legendary outlaw, Belle Starr, the Bandit Queen, who was popularized in many books and movies. Born Myra Belle Shirley in southwest Missouri, she was the daughter of wealthy parents who owned considerable land and many slaves. Considered a brilliant child, she was educated at an exclusive girls' academy and became an accomplished musician. But in time, her main interest centered around guns and horses. She became an expert horsewoman and deadly shot with either pistol or rifle.

Belle's family was strongly devoted to the Southern cause and supported the ruthless rebel leader, Quantrell. She idolized Cole Younger and the James brothers, viewing them as dashing heroes in Quantrell's band of raiders. As a spy, she provided information on Union detachments, reportedly enabling the Confederacy to capture a $1,500,000 supply train; and Belle occasionally encountered a Union spy, (Wild) Bill Hickcock.

After the war, Belle's father moved the family to Texas. In 1867, Cole Younger, his brothers, and the James brothers visited the Shirley ranch after committing their first bank robbery. Allegedly, when the gang left, Belle was pregnant with Younger's child.

Another story relates that Belle married a childhood friend, Jim Reed, who she had known as a Quantrell raider, and bore his child (Pearl). Reed, the son of a wealthy Missouri farmer, had migrated to Texas and became an obscure but proficient horse thief. As a member of a large band of horse thieves, he introduced Belle to the business of stealing horses. Business was highly profitable until his brother was slain by a rival gang. Jim hunted down and killed those responsible. When warrants were issued for his arrest and a large reward offered for his capture, he fled into the Territory and took up residence at the Tom Starr ranch, a haven for fugitives and outlaws.

A local deputy sheriff in Texas named John Morris tracked him down and killed him, presumably for the reward. Belle's response is described as follows:

> *When she received word to come and take charge of her husband's dead body, her eyes took a hard look and she said, They've killed him for the reward but they will never get it, and rode to the house where the body lay. Belle walked to the body, gave a glance at the face of her loved one and without the least sign of emotion, but with a scornful curve of the lips, quietly remarked: I am very sorry gentlemen, that you have made such a mistake and killed the wrong man; very sorry, indeed. John Morris, you will have to kill Jim Reed if you desire to secure the reward offered for Jim Reed's body.[3]*

Belle returned to the Starr Ranch and soon married the handsome Sam Starr, the son of Tom Starr. Now a citizen of the Cherokee Nation, Belle began her career as the notorious head of an effective band of horse thieves operating out of her ranch, known as Younger's Bend (after her lover, Cole Younger). She established elaborate horse-stealing centers approximately 50 miles apart, where horses from the north were exchanged for those stolen a similar distance to the south. A blacksmith who worked for her later claimed he sometimes nailed shoes on her horses backwards to deceive deputies.

***

How and when Bass met Belle Starr is not clear, although his interaction with her in the line of duty is documented.

The body of a known horse thief, John Middleton, had washed up down river near Fort Smith. The man had drowned; a horse, presumably his, was found upstream of the body. On the horse was a fancy saddle with the insignia of Belle Starr, but the brand on the horse was of A.G. McCarty. McCarty identified the horse as one stolen from him. The conclusion was that Belle Starr and John Middleton had been on a horse-stealing spree before Middleton drowned. Bass discovered this information while investigating Middleton's death. Securing a warrant for Starr's arrest, Bass went after her. What happened next is conjecture, what is known as fact is that once Bass found Belle, she relayed the truth of the matter to him. According to Belle, she and Middleton had bought the horse from a Fayette Barnett, not knowing that the animal was stolen. Bass investigated further and verified Belle's story. He advised her to give herself up and he would speak to Parker on her behalf. In a jury trial, Belle Starr was found guilty. Bass and Belle remained friends for the duration of Belle's life.

This was indeed an odd alliance. Belle Starr was a well-known Confederate sympathizer, and former slave owner. But there developed between the two, former slave and former slave owner, outlaw and lawman, a mutual respect and friendship.

Doctor Jesse Mooney was also a friend of Belle's. He was her personal physician as well as one of the first doctor in the Territory to perform a cesarean. Mooney kept a diary of his life in the Territory. The journal chronicled the many colorful people that he met, including Bass Reeves. Charles W. Mooney wrote about his father meeting Bass at Belle Starr's home in Younger's Bend. Mooney related:

THE TIES THAT BIND

While Dr. Jesse and Ella were visiting with Belle Starr one Sunday afternoon, the loud barking of Belle's Great Dane warned them someone was approaching. Soon, a lone rider came into view. He was a big, broad shouldered man, riding high in his saddle, [he] was clean shaven except for a bushy mustache. As he rode into the clearing in front of Belle's house, they saw he was a Negro wearing a Deputy U.S. Marshal's badge pinned on his shirt.

"It's Bass Reeves," Belle said, as she walked out of her cabin door and called off the dog. "Howdy, Miss Belle," the Deputy said politely, dismounting.

"What brings you this way, Reeves?" Belle asked.

"Jest ridin' through and thought I'd stop, but didn't know you had company."

"That's alright, Reeves, you're welcome any time yore near here. This is Doc Mooney and his wife Ella," Belle said.

"Pleased to meetcha'," the Deputy responded, tipping his hat politely. "Yore Uncle Isaac told me about you, Doctor. I've know'd him a long time."

"Reeves here is one of the few Deputy Marshals I trust," Belle remarked to Jesse and Ella. "He's been a friend of mine for several years ..."

"Just thought I'd warn you," the Deputy said, "I'm on the trail of Bob and Grat Dalton. They might be headed this way."

> *"Much a-blidged, Reeves. But them rascals won't be comin' round here for no help. Bob Dalton knows what I think of him,"* Belle remarked.

When Bass left, Belle told her guests that it was unusual for her, a Confederate sympathizer, to be a Negro's friend. But she respected his courage, fearlessness and willingness to "shoot it out" if necessary.[4]

The depth of the relationship between Belle Starr and Bass Reeves is lost to history. In his later years, Bass was unwilling to divulge the exact nature of the friendship, saying that he enjoyed visiting with her at Younger's Bend whenever he could, and that she was always a lady.

Less than a year after Bass met Doc Mooney at Younger's Bend, Belle was shot in the back as she rode near her home. The killer was never caught.

CHAPTER **NINE**
Rumors, Repudiation And Reputation

In performing his duties, Bass killed at least 14 men and claimed he never drew first in a gunfight. In each instance, however, he killed only to keep from being killed. Judge Parker always demanded a thorough investigation of any deaths that occurred during an arrest. If the evidence warranted, a deputy would be charged with murder. In one case, Parker sentenced a deputy to three years in the penitentiary, because he did more shooting than was justified in an attempt to make an arrest. Although Parker understood that some of his deputies could not bear careful scrutiny, he tolerated some of their shortcomings as long as they served the cause of justice. He figured a coward could be highly moral, but he could not be a deputy in the Indian Territory.

By 1882, seven years after he was sworn in, Bass Reeves had earned a reputation as a cunning and highly effective Deputy Marshal. He was a natural tracker. His rapport with the Indians in the Territory, as well as his reputation as an honest man, helped him capture a high percentage of the outlaws he went after. However, along with his reputation came rumors and accusations. Many sought to discredit Bass at every opportunity. To say that he had to have a thick skin to survive would be an understatement. Throughout it all, Bass continued to do his job; however, questions continued to crop up. Since Bass was involved in so many killings, questions sometimes arose about his arrest methods. A former resident of the Creek Nation claimed:

> *Reeves had the name of being a good officer and when he went after a man he got him. One time he went after two mean Negroes and knew when he left that if he didn't kill them, they would kill him for it would be impossible to bring them back alive. When he found them, they were lying under a tree asleep, but before he could get to them one awakened and got up. Reeves started talking to him and gave him a letter to read. By that time the other one was up. When the first had read the letter Reeves told him to let the other one read it. When he turned to give the letter to the other one, Reeves shot him and then the second before he could draw. That looks like a cold blooded murder to us now but it was really quick thinking and bravery.[1]*

Another settler claimed that Bass ... "many times ... never brought in all the criminals that he arrested but would kill some of them. The reasoning was that Bass didn't want to spend time chasing down men that resisted arrest, so he would shoot him down in his tracks." Both accusations are contradictory, many times deputies were not paid for dead outlaws; in addition, the dead man's funeral expenses were often borne by the deputy. But for Bass Reeves the reasons that the accusations could never be true was that he believed strongly in reason and justice in the court, over the rule of the gun. Bass tried to avoid violence whenever possible. His disguises allowed him to avoid violent confrontations by taking desperados by surprise. Bass exercised unusual restraint in his desire to avoid killing unnecessarily. In the case of John Cudjo he used a great deal of restraint indeed.

Assigned to bring in John Cudjo, a horse thief, Bass learned that the man was holed up at his home in the Seminole Nation. Cudjo had been alerted and was expecting Bass as he approached the house. Later, at Cudjo's trial, Bass testified:

> *When he heard the horses coming he jumped up with his Winchester in his hands ... I jumped down off my horse and called him. I had a writ for him: Deft said he knew that but damn me; I could not serve it: By this time he had sent his wife and two children away from the house: Deft said he knew I had a writ for him that he never was going with me to Fort Smith: that this was his house that he built and for me to get off his land: I told him I had a writ for him and I was not going away without him one way or the other: he told me to get away from him ... that he was not going to go with any marshal, me nor any other damn son of a bitch of a marshal and me especially ... [he] told me to go away that he allowed (sic) to die right there at home. I told him government had not sent me out to kill him but to arrest him: I seen I could do nothing with him.[2]*

Aware that Cudjo was a married father of minor children, Bass sent for the accused man's wife and neighbor in one last attempt to convince him to surrender. Bass testified that they told Cudjo he was very foolish, and to put down his gun and go with him. Soon it was agreed that the neighbor would go in the house and not be harmed. A little later, Cudjo surrendered.

All in all, Bass reputation for fair treatment of his prisoners overshadowed the rumors. Perhaps that is why in April 1882, Bass was approached by a whiskey peddler, a Creek Indian named Lockharjo. Unlike many of the whiskey peddlers Bass arrested in the Territory, Lockharjo sought Bass out. Lockharjo confessed to introducing two gallons of whiskey into the Indian area the Christmas before. He wanted to surrender himself to Bass. It is not clear why Lockharjo surrendered, possibly because he knew that Bass was in the Territory and would eventually hunt him down.

Bass sent a telegram from the Seminole agency dated April 11, 1882:

> *Please have a writ issued for Lockharjo a Creek Indian for introducing two gallons of whiskey into the Indian Territory last Christmas. He came up and acknowledged to the crime and wants to ... stand hi trial ... Please issue the writ and hold it in the office for I am afraid I will miss the writ if you send it. I will be in Fort Smith on the first of May.*[3]

Bass requested Marshal Boles to prepare a writ for Lockharjo He wanted the writ held in Fort Smith because he was afraid if it was sent back to him in the Territory, he might miss it. He planned to be back in Fort Smith the first of May. Jinney was pregnant again and Bass hoped for a boy. The baby was due sometime at the end of the summer and Bass wanted to be home.

In the past seven years, Bass had witnessed justice in many forms. Some of the prisoners that he brought in were tried, convicted and sentenced to hang. Other outlaws were convicted but shown mercy by the court. Judge Parker dealt justice with a fair hand. Whenever Bass could have a hand in seeing that justice was served, he did so. Often Bass would go to Parker on behalf of a suspect that he had brought in. Because of his detective skills and penchant for investigating the alleged crimes, Bass usually brought in substantial evidence along with his prisoners. In everything that he did in his career, Bass sought justice—as was the case of three boys accused of murder.

Bass arrested the three young Creek boys for the murder of a White man. One of the boys was named Luce Hammon. After talking with the boys and hearing their version, Bass was not entirely sure that they had actually committed the crime. Once the boys were delivered to the Fort Smith jail, Bass discussed the matter with Judge Parker.

The facts disclosed that a number of shots had been fired one night into the camp of a White man named Owens. One of the shots struck Owens in the thigh. Owens later died from the wound. Although the evidence against the boys seemed not enough for a conviction, the jury nonetheless found the boys guilty of murder which was a hanging offense. On the strength of the evidence that Bass had presented to him, Judge Parker sent a request to the President of the United States asking him to commute the mandatory death sentences.

In commuting the sentences to life imprisonment, President Grover Cleveland cited the facts that had been brought to the attention of the court by Bass. The President noted:

> *Whereas it appears that his crime was committed four years ago when the said Luce Hammon was a mere youth, and during the existence of factional war in the Creek Nation when the customary*

restraints of law were relaxed and the example of older Indians had an evil influence on the actions of their boys.[4]

Luck passed down this favorite story of Uncle Bass about the compassion of Judge Parker. Sahquahnee, a Sac and Fox Indian, was arrested for murder. Sahquahnee had been to a tribal celebration; and, when he returned to his village, he joined several friends in a discussion of the White man. The more the men talked, the angrier they became, filling their hearts with a renewed hatred of all Whites. It was alleged that they stalked and killed a White man insisting the White man was their enemy and it was not wrong to kill him.

Judge Parker sentenced Sahquahnee to die on the gallows. Sahquahnee was asked if he believed in God. Puzzled, he asked who God was, and the interpreter explained. "I have not heard of him," Sahquahnee replied, "but I have heard of the Great Spirit in the sky who loves my people." Even though he had killed, it seemed to Bass and Judge Parker that the gallows were not a just end for Sahquahnee. To the surprise of everyone, Judge Parker petitioned U. S. President Chester A. Arthur to commute the death sentence.

Despite evidence to the contrary, Bass was officially accused of mistreating his prisoners. The accusations came at a time in his life when he should have counted himself a lucky and blessed man. He had a son.

On August 4, 1882 Benjamin Reeves was born. Named after the benefactor of his grandfather, Ben entered the world on the heels of rumors and accusations intended to discredit his father. Bass scarcely had time to enjoy the birth of his son.

Information had been brought to the Marshal's office implicating Bass in the blackmail and abuse of his prisoners. Allegedly Bass extorted fifty cents from each prisoner that he captured. Supposedly, he would use the money to buy tobacco.

Those prisoners that refused to pay were whipped by the other prisoners.[5]

Bass was suspended pending an investigation. Though it meant that he could spend time with his new son, Bass was preoccupied with proving his innocence. Upon further investigation, it was found that the whipping that took place was highly exaggerated and not performed by Bass at all. It would seem that the prisoners themselves were having a little fun with a new prisoner. The investigation proved that Bass had not been involved in the incident and he was reinstated.

Those who knew Bass never doubted that he was innocent. He had a reputation for being a highly principled man who always treated his fellow man with compassion, be they prisoners or not. Though he had been found innocent of the blackmail and abuse charges, rumors still persisted. In the same year that he had been accused of mistreating his prisoners, Bass was involved in three deaths. The first death was the accidental shooting of his cook.

In April 1884, Bass, cook/guard William Leach, and wagon driver Johnnie Brady were transporting five prisoners to Fort Smith from the Chickasaw Nation. One of the prisoners, a Jim Grayson, was ill and accompanied by his wife. After the evening meal, Bass, Brady, and Leach were seated around the campfire. Grayson and his wife were nearby. The other prisoners were in a tent. Customarily, in the evening before leaving camp, Bass checked his ammunition and cleaned and loaded his guns, so that he could arrive at his destination before daybreak. This evening he was preparing to leave in search of two outlaws he believed were in the vicinity. As he tried to eject a cartridge stuck in his rifle, it went off, the bullet striking Leach fatally in the neck.

The second two deaths occurred while riding the Seminole whiskey trail and closing in on his man. Bass was ambushed by three brothers named Brunter for whom he was also searching.[6] The brothers, who were wanted for murder, horse stealing and robbery, believed that Bass was hot on their trail. But now they had him. He was ordered to dismount and keep his hands away from his guns. Bass began a casual conversation, showing the brothers the warrants he carried for their arrests and asking them trivial questions as if seeking information for purposes of reporting the incident. Totally surprised and amused by the lawman's conduct under the circumstances, one outlaw laughed and the others relaxed their guard for only an instant. It was all that Bass needed. With lighting speed, he drew his .45, killing two instantly. While holding the gun barrel of the third one—who got off three wild shots—Bass finally struck him over the head with his .45.

Each of the three deaths were investigated by Parker as was routine. In each case Bass was found innocent of any wrongdoing.

***

Throughout his career Bass struggled with the notion of justice. He had to admit that some of the rules, imposed at times by different Marshals of the court, seemed not only unjust, but also downright foolish, even dangerous. This included a directive that prohibited the use of a prisoner's horse, gun or bullets, even in life and death situations. The rule made no sense to Bass and was one of the reasons that Bass sometimes chose to work out of other jurisdictions. Another reason for working in other regions was the fact that, from time to time, the court at Fort Smith had to suspend operations because of a lack of funds. This was a major frustration for Bass and the other deputies. Fort Smith was the largest criminal court in the country, handling more than 1,000 criminal cases annually. The court costs and witness fees were among the nation's highest. Bass had trouble wrapping his mind around the fact that a government could run out of money for law enforcement.

With the arrest of each outlaw, Bass felt that he was making the world safer for his children. He doubted more and more that

Jinney would ever realize her dream of raising their children in the Territory. He has seen more of the Territory than his wife had these past seven years. The home that Jinney longed for was all but gone. He was convinced that his children would never grow up in the Territory, a feeling that he kept to himself. That his children would grow up free and have chances that he never had was enough for Bass. He and Jinney both wanted their children to go to school, be educated. Bass thought of a son who could be a lawyer, maybe even a judge. A son, who like his father, would spend his life in the service of justice. The girl Alice was a quiet child. Jinney planned for her to be a teacher. That would also make him proud. Bass believed that with God all things were possible.

***

Of the many gun battles during his career, none were more memorable than his encounter with Bob Dozier. The outlaw had provoked Bass for several years, even though they met face to face only once.

Dozier had been a prosperous farmer for years; however, he found the wild criminal life so appealing that he deliberately abandoned his peaceful farm life to become an outlaw. Dozier believed in diversification of his criminal activity, he found it safer and profitable. In accordance, Dozier stole cattle and horses, robbed stores and banks, hijacked cattle buyers carrying large sums of money, held up stage coaches, ambushed travelers, stuck up big money poker games, participated in land swindles and other confidence activities. Along the way, he killed several people and reportedly tortured others to obtain information needed for his operations.

With diversification in mind, Dozier carefully avoided goading any one particular group of people into banding together to aid federal marshals seeking his arrest. Nearly everyone knew that he always remembered a favor and never forgot a traitor.

Hence, the marshals were hamstrung for years trying to locate and arrest him. When Bass joined the chase, he knew what the outlaw looked like from victim's descriptions. He also understood Dozier's escape strategies. Bass decided that a lone-wolf pursuit, aided by a one-man posse, would accomplish more than a team of deputies. But for several months, Bass' efforts to arrest Dozier failed. At one point, the outlaw sent word to Bass that if he did not stop hounding him, he was as good as dead. Bass sent word back that at least Dozier would have to quit running to kill him, and he was ready at any time to give the outlaw his chance.

Before Bass got a chance to pit his wits against Dozier, he found himself on the trail of another equally as challenging outlaw, Jim Webb.

Jim Webb was a cowboy from Brazos, Texas. Webb had the reputation of being a top cattle hand and a dangerous man. Webb drifted into the Chickasaw Nation and decided to remain. He found employment with a popular rancher, Billy Washington, who was a partner with Dick McLish, a prominent Chickasaw Indian. As ranch foreman, Webb supervised 45 tough cowboys. Those he could not whip with his fists, he fired. Webb was an argumentative bully who used his fists and guns to make his point. As far as Jim Webb was concerned, he was a law unto himself.

One day William Steward, a circuit preacher whose farm bordered the Washington-McLish ranch, ran afoul of Webb. Steward set a grass fire on his own farm (probably in preparation for planting). The fire spread to the Washington-McLish ranch. Webb confronted the preacher. Steward apparently did not appreciate what Webb had to say. Words were exchanged and a bitter, brief quarrel ended with Steward's death. Bass was assigned to bring Webb in. Bass hired Floyd Wilson as his posse-man and the chase was on.

Several days later, Bass and Wilson reached the Washington-McLish ranch around 8:00 a.m. As they approached the ranch house, only Webb, a cowboy named Frank Smith, and the ranch cook were present. Bass and Wilson rode up like traveling cowboys and asked for breakfast. Webb, however, was suspicious. As Bass and Wilson walked up to the porch, both Webb and Smith held their guns nonchalantly at their sides, ready for trouble. Bass wondered how he might arrest Webb without getting killed. He and Wilson were told to wait in the kitchen-dining room side of the ranch house until the cook could prepare their breakfast.

Bass asked if he could feed his horses while waiting for breakfast. Granting permission with a grunt, Webb followed the lawman out to the barn, eyeing him every second, gun still in hand. Talking easily, steadily, without revealing his uneasiness, Bass fed the horses, loosened their saddle girths, and casually pulled his Winchester from his saddle boot. He leaned it against a corn crib, hoping to convince Webb that he was honestly just a cowboy passing through.

After eating, Bass and Wilson walked out into the "dog run" followed by Webb, who stood directly over the Deputy Marshal as he settled on a bench. Smith and Wilson sat at the opposite end. Webb and Smith, guns still in hand, watched Bass and Wilson silently. Bass had no chance to signal Wilson. Talking on, he hoped for the right moment to strike his blow.

The stalemate continued as Bass kept up his aimless conversation. A dog on a neighboring ranch began howling piteously and other dogs chimed in. Webb's attention was diverted from Bass for only a second. The lawman leaped to his feet, knocked Webb's gun away, wrapped his left arm around the outlaw's throat, drew his own gun with his right hand and shoved it into Webb's face. He gurgled out a meek surrender.

Surprised by the sudden attack, Wilson did not try to seize Smith who fired two shots at Bass, both missing. With Webb completely controlled by his left hand, Bass fired one shot. Smith fell to the ground, the fight burned out of him by a .45 slug in his abdomen. Still gripping Webb's throat, Bass instructed Wilson to handcuff Webb, then mapped plans to return his prisoners to the court in Paris, Texas.

Webb and the wounded Smith were loaded into a two-horse wagon, and the long return trip began. En route, Smith died from his wounds and was buried without ceremony. Reaching Paris, Bass jailed Webb then forgot about him. But they were destined to meet again. For the moment, he had other fish to fry. Bass headed for the Territory and back on the trail of Bob Dozier.

***

He had picked up Dozier's trail in the upper Cherokee Nation. In hot pursuit, Bass Reeves' large powerful hands gripped the reins as he urged his horse on. His six foot 200 plus body was taut with tension as he concentrated on catching Dozier. Sweat and steam from the horse mixed with the sweat of the man. Adrenaline pumped through both man and animal. The wind pushed the black handle bar moustache against Reeves' brown skin, as trained eyes scoured the ground and the trees. Bass knew he was close. Dozier had eluded lawmen for years. But now Reeves was only hours behind the fugitive. Looking back once to make sure his posse-man was keeping up, Bass Reeves leaned forward in the saddle and concentrated on his prey. They rode deeper and deeper into the Cherokee Hills, closing the gap between lawman and outlaw. Dozier and an unknown accomplice were just out of his reach, but not for long. Bass was determined to bring in Dozier, this time.

Day was turning into night and still Bass pressed on. As long as he could see Dozier's tracks, he'd keep riding. But Mother Nature seemed to be on the other side of justice. Lightning and thunder made the eerie Cherokee

Hills even more foreboding. A heavy downpour began washing away the tracks of the outlaw's horses. Suspending hope of tracking Dozier any further, Bass and his one-man posse looked for a dry place to camp for the night. Ahead lay a wide, heavily timbered ravine; using lightning flashes to find their way, they rode down treacherous slopes. The horses fought to gain footing on the muddy ground. Just as they reached the bottom of the ravine, a gun shot rang out, the slug whining past Bass' head.

Jumping from their horses, Bass and his posse sought cover in the nearby trees. Hearts pounding they waited, expecting more shots. Instead a man's dim shadow slipped from tree to tree. Bass crouched low, not moving. He waited until the shadow was caught between two trees, quickly he fired two shots. The shadow jerked back once and fell. One man was down. Almost simultaneously, the other outlaw fired on Bass. The lawman stood upright clutching his chest, he took a reeling step away from the protective trees and fell face first to the ground. For several minutes, the ravine was quiet except for the rain and thunder. Bass lay in the mud, fully exposed. Within minutes, a man stepped from behind a tree, looked at Bass lying on the ground, and burst into laughter. Lightning outlined the man's face revealing Bob Dozier. The outlaw gloated over the inert body of Bass Reeves. His gun at his side, he casually stepped closer to the body of his nemesis. When he was just a few yards away, the inert body came to life. A very much alive Bass was now looking at Dozier, gun in hand. The deputy ordered Dozier to surrender. Frozen in surprise, Dozier hesitated a moment, then dropped to a crouching position as he fired his gun. But Bass was too quick, he shot his gun as he rolled to the side. The lawman's bullet buried itself in Dozier's neck, instantly killing him. Breathing hard, Bass waited for movement from Dozier. Cautiously he stood, all the while keeping his eye trained on the still form. He wasn't going to make the same mistake the unfortunate outlaw had made. Seeing no movement, his gun still cocked, Bass moved swiftly, knocking the gun out of Dozier's hand and turned the body over with his boot. Dozier was dead. Bass took a deep breath and said to himself, "Not tonight, Reba. Not tonight."

Bass was determined to claim only part of Reba's prophecy. Yes, he had seen plenty of danger in his life. As a lawman sworn to bring justice and peace to the Indian Territory, Bass Reeves faced danger more days than not. As a Deputy Marshal he was indeed a leader. But he had promised his wife that he'd do everything in his power not to "die a fore his time." Bass told his daughter that he considered his encounter with Bob Dozier one of the high points of his career, because he had succeeded where so many others had failed.

Although the Fort Smith Elevator failed to report the clash between Bass and Webb, the newspaper was quick to implicate Bass in the wrongdoing of his posse-man in another matter. On October 17, 1884, it reported that:

> *Bass Reeves, one of the most successful of the marshals doing business in the Territory, had been discharged from the force by Marshal Boles. It seems he had a habit of letting a prisoner escape when more could be made than in holding him and that is where the trouble came in.*

Bass denied the accusations and there are no records to indicate he was discharged or relieved of duty. Certainly, there was no evidence produced to support the newspaper's innuendo. It was reported that Frank Pierce, acting as a posse-man for Bass, was a notorious horse thief and that Bass was with him. Later, Pierce was killed in a fight between Texas officers and cattle thieves from the nation.

***

While Bass continued to track criminals and bring them to justice, his children were growing. Both Ben and Alice attended a new grade school for Negroes in Fort Smith. The illiterate Deputy Marshal had been pleased that both of his children enjoyed school work. The Reeves' children received more schooling then the average child because their mother continued to teach them in the home. Jinney took pride in the fact that her children had good command of the English language. She insisted that each child speak properly. Throughout the years, there became a marked distinction between the way Bass spoke and the way his children and wife spoke. With his lack of formal education, Bass' grammar and word usage was limited. However, Bass was eager for his children (Ben especially) to secure first a formal education then a career, hopefully as a lawyer to help people with laws that would surely outlive the gun. In short, Ben was to be an educated and refined gentleman rather than a rough-hewed frontiersman like his father. Though as the boy grew he seemed more embarrassed by his father than anything. Alice, on the other hand, looked up to her father. In later years, she would fondly tell stories that demonstrated Bass' dedication and resourcefulness.

CHAPTER **TEN**
The Trial

In 1886, the efforts to discredit Bass and remove the tin star from his chest seemed to finally pay off. During the February 1886 term of court and immediately after U. S. Attorney Clayton left office, a grand jury indicted Bass for murder, finding that he feloniously, willfully and of his malice and forethought did mortally wound William Leach (the cook), who then and there instantly died.

It was totally unexpected. Bass had thought the incident closed. He was especially chagrined that the old rumors and lies were now being treated as fact. The popular version of the shooting, apparently originating with the prisoners, was later perpetuated by scholars and newspapers alike. This version held that the cook had thrown hot grease on Bass' dog and the Deputy Marshal became so enraged that he shot the cook. The story goes on to say that the cook fell into the campfire, and Bass refused to allow anyone to remove his body until it was charred black.

The grand jury's action was precipitated by concerted efforts to publicly disgrace Bass and force his resignation or dismissal. Court records indicate that Deputy Marshal G.J.B. Fair secured a warrant for Bass' arrest on January 18, 1886.* Learning of the warrant, the *Arkansas Gazette* (Little Rock) of January 22, 1886, immediately published a totally inaccurate account of Bass' arrest:

Caught Up With
An Ex-Deputy Marshal's Misdeeds Brought to Light

Ex-Deputy United States Marshal Bass Reeves was arrested and lodged in jail today, charged with the murder of Wm. Leach, in the Chickasaw nation, in April, 1884. Leach was cooking at Reeves' camp when the murderous official shot him dead for some trivial offense. Reeves has been constantly on the marshal's force here for several years, and notwithstanding rumors reached here frequently that he was in league with some of the worst cutthroats and outlaws in the Indian country, he managed to cover up his tracks so effectively as to retain his commission until the recent marshal took charge, when he was removed. During his long service as an official, he has stained his hands with the blood of his fellow beings, and now languishes in jail with many others whom he has been instrumental in placing there. One of

---

*On December 10, 1886, representatives of the Department of Justice recommended Deputy Fair's immediate removal from office presenting false accounts in an unrelated matter.

The Trial

the witnesses to the killing of Leach is now in prison at Detroit, where he was sent for some minor offense, but his pardon will be asked for in order that his testimony in the case may be taken.

Bass was relieved of his duties and had to post a $3,000 bond to remain free pending trial. Several of his friends, including Deputy James H. Mershon, who was mentioned earlier, insisted on signing as sureties. Mershon, was perhaps the more efficient of the men who rode for Parker,* (one of his cases was adapted to film in True Grit, starring John Wayne). William Clayton, the U. S. Attorney at the time of the occurrence, also signed the bond. Both Mershon and Clayton were aware of a public vendetta against Bass. Before concluding that the Leach shooting was an accident, Clayton had interviewed each of the persons in the camp at the time of the shooting. Some prisoners, however, were induced to change their stories from initial accounts they gave to Clayton and Marshal Boles. The later versions were the basis for the indictment.

Before his trial began, Bass was approached on the street by A. J. Boyd, an impaneled juryman expected to hear his case. Addressing him as "You Black son of a bitch," he informed Bass that "Me and three others [jurymen] have it in for you. It's the way about you, the way you walk, and the clothes you wear, like you was somebody and some of us don't amount to much." Extremely angry but realizing any retaliation would subject him to further serious charges, he took the matter directly to Judge Parker. Then Bass filed a formal complaint with the court, explaining:

I was standing ... on the sidewalk a few days ago ... when A. J. Boyd came up to me and tapped me on the shoulder with his walking cane, and asked me

---
*Mershon went insane in 1898.

how it was about that killing and said he wanted me to tell him about that killing and all about my case. I said to him, "You are a jury man and I have no statement to make until I go to the stand, and more than that I have no business talking to you about my case." He said, "Yes I am a jury man and if you want to save your neck you had better make a statement to me." I told him again I had no statement to make, he then said "You damned Black son of a bitch, I am just as certain to break your neck as I have this cane in my hand. Me and three others have got it in for you." I turned to walk away and he caught me by the coat and led me off of the sidewalk and said, "Now you had just as well tell me about your case" and I again told him I did not want to talk to him. I turned to walk away again when he raised his cane and shook it at me and said, "God damn you" ... I walked away. Dave Pompey, Phil Cyrus and John Williams overheard all or part of the conversation. Other persons were also nearby and perhaps overheard.[1]

Pompey and Williams verified Bass' version of the incident. Judge Parker promptly ordered Boyd to show cause why he should not be held in contempt for violating his specific orders. Boyd responded ambiguously:

In The Matter of Contempt of This Honorable Court, Alleged Against This Respondent, Upon The Information of One Bass Reeves, Respondent A. J. Boyd Comes Into Court And Answers, as Follows:

He states that he was a juror on the regular panel for the August term 1886 of this court. But he denies positively that he was willfully guilty of conduct violative of the instructions given by the court to him and the balance of the panel for the August term 1886, at the opening (illegible), as charged. In further response, the said A. J. Boyd states, that it is possible that he approached the said Bass Reeves and, as a juror, used improper words, but he denies all consciousness of having done so—and, if he did have such improper communication with the said Bass Reeves, he states positively he did not do so knowingly and willfully. But he believes that if any communications or conversation was had between him and the said Bass Reeves about the case pending in this court on the said Bass Reeves, that the said Bass Reeves approached him and was (illegible). He states, in further reply and explanation, that unfortunately some years ago he acquired an appetite for intoxicants, which at times is very strong and violent. And that after taking several drinks his mind becomes a blank. That prior to the alleged misconduct, in seeking to have improper conversation with the said Bass Reeves, he had abstained from drinking intoxicating liquors for the period of about fifteen months. That he did not drink anything while a juror as aforesaid, until about the date said for the conversation with said Bass Reeves. But he states that about the time of the alleged meeting with said Bass Reeves he was drinking heavily, and commenced to do so against his will, but his will-

power was not serving enough to resist the appetite for whiskey that at periods assails him.

He knows nothing whatsoever about the conversation detailed as occurring between himself and said Reeves, and as to the same his mind is a blank—and he notes if anything was said that he ought not as a juror to have said, it was not willful, nor was he conscious of what he was doing or saying. With this answer, he submits himself to the orders of the court.[2]

Judge Parker found Boyd guilty of contempt for violating his specific instructions to all juryment and immediately sentenced him to serve time in the Fort Smith jail.

Finally, on October 12, 1887, more than a year after Bass' arrest and two and one-half years after the incident, the trial began.[3] In due course, Bass testified in detail that his rifle had gone off accidentally and the bullet killed Leach. He stated:

Before I would start anywhere when I was out on a trip I would always examine my cartridges and gun and that night in examining my gun I found I had a .45 cartridge in the magazine and I couldn't throw it up in the barrel. I was down on my knee and had the Winchester laying up this way (shows by holding Winchester in position, etc.). I reached my hand in my coat pocket and got my knife and put my hand back this way and either my knife or hand struck the trigger and the gun went off (shows by getting down to the jury and laying the gun across his left arm the muzzle pointing about 45 degrees). The gun went off then and the boy hallooed and said, 'Lordy, you have hit Leach.'

The Trial

***

Q Where was your gun lying when you picked it up?
A In the scabbard. I had been working with the gun some 3 or 4 minutes when it went off. I was trying to prize this .45 cartridge out with my knife. I had thrown out some cartridges.
Q When you found you had shot him, what did you do?
A I throwed down the gun and told Jim Grayson to come and help pick him up and I took my handkerchief out and soused it in a bucket of water and put it on his neck.
Q Did you intend to shoot him?
A No sir.
Q There was something said about a dog. What was it?
A He was running around there and I said, 'You had better kill that dog, it is some little Indian dog and you had better kill it,' and I never looked up. We hadn't had any words at all. He was all the help I had to work for me. Wilson was 30 miles behind. There was Johnnie and you couldn't trust him with 5 prisoners in that country no how, you can't hardly trust yourself.
Q Did it bleed much?
A No sir.
Q What did Jim do?
A He come right at once and we picked him up and I made a bed in the tent and him and me carried him in there.
Q Did he complain much that night?
A No sir. I then put Jim [Grayson] on my horse and told him to go after old man Nat [Doctor Nathan Cochran] quick.

Grayson was unable to return with the doctor, and it was the next day before Leach received medical attention. While the gunshot wound was serious, it was not considered life threatening. Bass left Leach with a doctor, who he instructed to bill him for Leach's medical costs. It was understood that Leach would remain with the doctor until he recovered.

Bass' 14-year-old nephew, Johnnie Brady(the author's uncle), appeared before the grand jury and was initially listed as a witness for the prosecution since he was the only other person at the camp fire when the shooting occurred. But his testimony, as well as that of Mary Grayson, wife of the prisoner who assisted Bass after the accident, confirmed Bass' version of the accident. Johnnie testified that:

> *Bass got his gun and was putting a cartridge in it and it went off and shot Leach. Defendant said there I have shot Leach but didn't aim to do it. I aimed to kill the dog. Bass sent for a doctor, but could not get any that night, and next morning, he took him to a doctor and told him to care for him if he could and that he would pay the bill, and if he got well to get a hack and send him home and that he would pay all the bills.*

> *Bass gun was a .44 caliber Winchester rifle. He had been working with his gun trying to get a cartridge out that was too big. I think he was on one knee working with his gun when it went off. I asked Leach if he was badly hurt and he said he was, and that he didn't believe that Bass shot him on purpose. They had always been perfectly friendly. Leach was shot in the neck. I had Leach tell the doctor that he did not think Bass shot him on purpose. I had been with Bass and Leach on the trip about two months and I never heard a cross word between them.*

Mary Grayson, who had accompanied her husband (a prisoner at the time of the shooting) related that just prior to the shooting:

Q They was just having a friendly conversation were they?
A Yes sir.
Q Reeves appeared to be in a good humor?
A Yes sir.
Q If he was angry you didn't discover it?
A No sir.
Q You didn't hear him use an angry word, did you?
A No sir.
Q When the gun fired, how long had he been fixing the gun he was squatting down by the fire loading it wasn't he?
A No sir, he had laid it down. He was picking out the cartridges with his pocket knife.
Q They were hung in the chamber and he was picking them out with his pocket knife?
A Yes sir, looked like it to me.

She declared that Bass, when Leach was shot, called for Jim and he sent Jim after a doctor.

Q Did Jim get the doctor that night?
A No sir. He got back about a day, I guess, I was asleep.... He couldn't get any doctor.

The testimony of the nine other witnesses, all having been arrested by Bass, did not vary substantially from Bass' account. They obviously decided to be totally truthful to escape Judge Parker's wrath in case they were found guilty of perjury. Parker felt duty bound to uncover perjury and falsehood and bring to justice false accusers or false witnesses ... whether they are on the side of the government or against it. He had sternly lectured that he considered perjury "the vilest and most dangerous of crimes". One witness, Toby Hill (a Creek Indian), was a prisoner in the camp when Leach was killed. Hill testified before the grand jury as a prosecution witness and at trial through an interpreter. He stated that when Bass "[w]orked with the lever, the gun fired. After Leach fell, Bass and Grayson jumped and picked him up and laid him in the mouth of the tent where they attended the wound in his neck." This was the second time that Bass had brought Hill down to Fort Smith.

No testimony indicated that Bass intended to kill Leach. Bass also contended Leach's death was hastened because of weakness brought on by a digestive disorder. Testimony showed that several prisoners became ill because of food that Leach had cooked. He himself was sick for several days and was being treated at Cherokee town up to the day before the shooting.

A review of the facts in the case reveals the unusual nature of its prosecution. The substance of the testimony of Ms. Grayson, as well as John Brady, was obviously known prior to the trial. Their version of what happened could hardly support a conviction for murder. Certainly, the prosecution was not prepared to show a violent dispute or even ill will between Bass and William Leach. Indeed, there was no basis upon which to show the shooting was intentional, willful or with malice and forethought. Moving to provide immediate assistance to Leach, Bass' conduct was inconsistent with one involved in a willful and intentional shooting. If, in fact, he intended to kill Leach with his rifle, death no doubt would have been instantaneous. It would also appear unreasonable to proceed with the prosecution of a case based solely on the prisoners' testimony. The prosecutor, as well as the court personnel, was surely aware of how anxious prisoners are to get even with an arresting officer.

The trial lasted three days ending on Saturday morning, October 15, and the case went to the jury. Paralee, insisted on being driven to Fort Smith each day. She wanted to see and hear

The Trial

everything that transpired as if her presence would assure a favorable outcome. Other family members attended court when they could—except Jinney. Since Bass' encounter with A. J. Boyd before the trial, she had been visibly ill from worry. After church on Sunday morning, Bass, his family and friends returned to the courthouse and remained that day. At 7:00 p.m., Edward Hunt, jury foreman, read the verdict to a crowded courtroom. "We the jury find the defendant not guilty as charged in the ... indictment." *The Fort Smith Elevator* (October 21, 1887) reported:

> *Bass Reeves was perhaps the best pleased man in Arkansas last Sunday when a verdict was announced pronouncing him innocent of the charge of murder ... His broad smiles attested his inward delight and in addition to shaking hands with the entire jury he worked Judge Parker's arm like a pump handle and assured him that he believed the trial would make him a better man.*

On the contrary, the stressful episode had taken its toll on Bass. He was particularly saddened that the charges were based on perjury on both sides of the law. But he understood that following his indictment, a full hearing was necessary because of Judge Parker's insistence on maintaining the integrity of his court. Ironically, the tragic incident was not associated with the capture of a desperate criminal.

But as a forceful and commanding Black law officer, he was an anomaly for the times and was seen by many as totally unacceptable. Despite the urging of family and friends that he resign, Bass' faith in the rule of law remained intact. He would not be swayed from serving the cause of justice; he immediately resumed his duties.

Right after the trial, false accounts of the circumstances circulated. *The Indian Chieftain* of October 20, 1887, reported:

> *Bass Reeves, the Negro marshal who has been on trial for murdering a prisoner, was acquitted a few days ago.*

Many years later, the *Muskogee Times-Democrat* on November 19, 1909, stated:

> *He (Reeves) then shot a man whom he was trying to arrest and was tried for murder. The fight for life in the courts was a bitter one but finally Reeves was acquitted on the testimony of a young Negro girl.*

With the trial behind him and his badge once again pinned on his vest, Bass returned to his duties. Riding back into the Territory as a lawman was probably therapeutic. Being a lawman was second nature to him. He was most comfortable when he was working. Besides, he had unfinished business to attend to. Jim Webb was on the loose.

Webb had spent nearly a year in jail when two friends arranged for his release on a $17,000 bond. Once out, Webb forfeited the bond rather than stand trial for murder. For two years he had remained free. Bass was determined to recapture him.

Finally, Bass received word that Webb had drifted back into the Chickasaw Nation and could be located at Jim Bywaters' general store. He then set out to investigate, taking John Cantrell with him as his posse. When Bass caught up with him, Webb made a classic last-ditch stand. He was determined not to be captured and face almost certain hanging. Webb fired his gun at Bass, the first bullet grazed the lawman's saddle horn. The second shot cut a button off of Bass' coat. Bass called to Webb to surrender, warning that he had no chance to escape. When Webb shot the bridle out of his hands, Bass lost control of his frightened horse. Ducking his head, he dove to the ground. As Bass rolled to his feet, Webb's fourth shot clipped the brim of his hat. The lawman drew his gun so fast that Webb had no time to aim his rifle for a fifth shot. The Deputy Marshal fired one shot from the hip, and Webb spun completely around, starting to fall. Before he landed on the ground, Bass hit him with two more shots. It was later discovered that all three bullets had hit Webb's body within a hand's width of each other.

By this time, Jim Bywaters and John Cantrell came running to the scene. They saw Webb dying on the ground, his revolver now in his hand, and they heard Webb feebly calling for Bass. Bass advanced a few wary steps toward the gunman, telling him to throw away his weapon. Webb hesitated a moment, then pitched it away, and the three men walked to the spot where the wounded outlaw law dying. Bywaters later wrote down Webb's last words on the back of a freight receipt. It was his farewell to the world. "Give me your hand, Bass. You are a brave, brave man. I want you to accept my revolver and scabbard as a present, and you must accept them. Take it, for with it I have killed eleven men, four of them in Indian territory, and I expected you to make the twelfth." Bass accepted the gifts; and in a few minutes, Webb breathed his last breath. Bass helped to bury him, then collected his boots to present them, along with the gun belt, as proof that the warrant had been served.[4] Bass later described Webb as "the bravest man he ever saw."

CHAPTER **ELEVEN**
Go West Young (White) Man

The year 1889 marked a turning point for the history of the Indian Territory. Bass Reeves and Judge Parker, whose lives were so inextricably involved, were no less affected. On February 6, Congress passed an act authorizing writs of error to the U.S. Supreme Court in all cases where there had been a conviction carrying a death sentence. The Act's primary aim was to provide a review of the numerous capital cases tried in Parker's court— thus ending Judge Parker's reign as the only American jurist whose decisions could not be appealed. Parker had no objection to appeal. He even favored abolition of the death penalty, provided there is a "certainty of punishment, whatever the punishment may be, for in the uncertainty of punishment following crime lies the weakness of our halting justice."

Depicted in newspapers across the country as "the Hanging Judge," Judge Parker had the reputation of being "heartless and blood thirsty. " His critics loudly proclaimed that in no civilized land should one man have the power to commit "judicial murder with no hope of appeal." In a speech before the U.S. House, the local Congressman declared that he did not want "the Judge Parker slaughter house in his district any longer." He acknowledged that Judge Parker "has done more to stay the progress of murder and crime in the Indian country than any other power" and his name was "a terror to evil doers." But he added, "while this court has been serving its purpose, it has done much to bring the good name of the city of Fort Smith and Western Arkansas into disrepute." For those more familiar with the conditions faced by the court, it was a different story. The change in the law was not viewed favorably in Fort Smith, as exemplified by the appeal of Cherokee Bill's conviction. *The Fort Smith Elevator* on September 13, 1895, expressed the consensus that if Cherokee Bill had been hung following his conviction for slaying Ernest Melton, he could not have murdered the popular jailor Lawrence Keating while attempting a jailbreak. It stated:

> *For the benefit of those who may not understand why Cherokee Bill was not hanged (why he was allowed to remain alive long enough to commit another brutal murder), we will say that his case was appealed to the Supreme Court of the United States upon what is known in law as technicalities— little instruments sometimes used by lawyers to protect the rights of litigants but oftener used to defeat the ends of justice. It will remain there until the bald-headed and big-bellied respectables who compose that body get ready to look into its merits.*

The Court's review of some of Parker's decisions pointed up the unique problems faced by the Fort Smith court. Since each Indian nation had its own system of laws, matters of citizenship required extensive explanation. Questions of jurisdiction arose over offenses involving Indians, Whites and Blacks which could not easily be determined. These included interpretation of treaties and laws relating to intermarriage and adoption. Slaves, freed under the treaties of 1866, provided a prime example. Those adopted by the Indians became Indians in the eyes of the law with attendant immunities. Evidence in criminal cases was therefore necessary to establish the allegation in an indictment that the defendant was "a White man and not an Indian." Or "a Negro and not an Indian," for if it was proved during the trial that the parties to the crime were Indians, either by blood, treaty, or adoption, the indictment was quashed.

Judge Parker's jury instructions on some of these thorny issues provided the basis for much contention with the court. He believed that the complex questions of law were beyond the knowledge and experience of rugged frontiersmen. This often led to the use of language and illustrations the high court believed constituted reversible error.

Congress, by an Act of March 1, continued to restrict the jurisdiction of Judge Parker and the dismantling of his court. The district court for Eastern Texas, located in Paris, was given jurisdiction over portions of the Choctaw and Chickasaw Nations. This legislation also established the first White man's court in the Territory at Muskogee. The new district court interfered with the Parker court to the extent that it was given exclusive, original jurisdiction of all offenses against the laws of the United States not punishable by death or imprisonment at hard labor. The court was clearly intended to provide a more convenient means of protecting the rights of White citizens. "A grievous mistake, a fearful blunder," said Judge Parker, realizing the court would use

White jurors of the region, almost ensuring that no Indian would get a break.

Following the Congressional action, President Harrison offered Judge Parker a much easier job as judge of the Eastern District of Arkansas. Parker declined the offer and, despite his diminished authority, felt his court was "one of more importance to the country."

Parker was highly indignant, however, at having borne alone the heavy burden placed on him by Congress for so long, which was now to be shared with the Supreme Court. Congress had known there were few laws and hardly any precedents for Parker to follow. In addition Parker was not compelled to follow state laws, but only the common law, which could be variously construed. Judge Parker had made his own rulings and established precedents that became law. While no other jurist in America has ever wielded so much power, he merely did what he was asked to do. Since he was vested with unlimited authority, he used it. Outspoken about the Congressional action, Judge Parker stated:

> *Back of this change is a maudlin sentimentality that condones a crime on which blood stains have dried. Take the good ladies who carry flowers and jellies to criminals. They mean well ... but, oh, what mistaken goodness! What motives of sincerity, piety and charity, sadly misdirected. They consider alone the prisoner chained in his cell ... the convict on the scaffold and his fatal plunge to death ... They forget the crime he perpetrated and the family he made husband less and fatherless by assassin's work.*[1]

When Congress limited the Fort Smith court's authority by placing jurisdiction over part of the southern Territory under the court in Paris, Texas, Bass volunteered for temporary duty. He had a personal reason for wanting to go to Paris. His birthplace, (the old plantation), was located in the general area. He had many times expressed an interest in going back there. Family history does not divulge whether or not he ever located the plantation. He did, however, serve the Paris court (which covered the southern part of the Territory) intermittently for several years.

During one of Bass' stints in Texas, a bitter dispute between a Black and a White farmer broke out leading to the killing of the Black man. Soon afterward, the White farmer's cattle and livestock were poisoned and his house set afire. In retaliation, several Black men were taken from their homes by Whites and hung. The sheriff arrested several Black men on charges of burning the house. White citizens in the area warned the sheriff that they planned to take his prisoners from jail. Because it was the jail that also housed federal prisoners, the sheriff asked the U.S. Marshal for protection. Bass was one of the deputies summoned. Though Bass and the other Marshals were successful in quelling the mob, Bass was deeply disturbed by the incident. It was his first experience with mob violence and the breakdown of the law; it was painfully apparent that the safety and rights of Black citizens had not even been considered.

Immediately upon his return, Bass had a long talk with Judge Parker about the rapidly changing times. By this time, Parker's power and prestige had diminished. And the wave of the future was nearly upon them. With the passage of the Congressional Act of March 2, 1889, the future barreled towards Bass and the Territory. That one piece of legislation opened White settlement to unassigned land in the Oklahoma district west of the Indian Territory. It was the beginning of the end of the Indian Territory.

On April 22, 1889, great crowds gathered on the borders of the unassigned land, while soldiers stood guard to turn back early invaders. At noon, they fired guns and blew bugles to signal people on foot, horseback and in wagons to commence their scramble for the sixty-acre homesteads. A U.S. cavalryman observed:

> *Riding to a high point of ground, where he could be seen for miles each way with a flag in one hand and a bugle in the other, the signal officer took his position. At precisely 12 o'clock he raised the bugle to his lips and gave the signal blast, long and loud, waving and dropping the flag at the same moment. Then began the race for homes ... It was a race free to all. None was barred. Neither sex, age, nor circumstances were imposed as conditions. The government was the starter, and the American people were the racers. Cheers and shouts from fifty thousand souls, a refrain to the bugle notes, sent their echoes o'er hill and plain, arousing into life the solitude of the en-chanting surroundings. The race began. The fleet racer and plow horse were given free rein, and plied with whip and spur. The long rail-way trains, too, with ear-piercing shrieks from their engine whistles, joined in the race. From the windows of every coach came shouts of cheer and the waving of flags and handkerchiefs to those that were racing to the south on either side of the fast-flying trains. The ranks of the racers were diminishing on every side; they were seen to leap from their horses; a happy shout, a waving of their hat, the setting of a flag or stake. They took a homestead. Oklahoma was the home of the White man.*[2]

Popular historians have glorified these early settlers as exemplars of America's true spirit and values, lauding them as legendary heroes of indomitable courage and individualism. Black men and women possessed of the same spirit, character and commitment came to this new land of opportunity for the same purpose. However, they generally were denied participation in the Land Rush. These settlers were challenged legally over reference to White settlements specified in the Congressional Act. Some were forced to abandon claims to choice land and relegated to scrub areas. Others, such as the Buffalo Soldier veterans, were financially able to fight successfully for their legal rights. But many were forced to return to their homes, mostly in the South. To Bass, the government's action in opening the land for White settlement and the subsequent mistreatment of Black settlers mocked the proclamations of freedom and justice and the hypocritical entreaties for Black citizens to lift themselves by their own bootstraps. It was an issue discussed in many of the Black homes. Children were probably present during these discussions. It would appear that Ben, though still relatively young, was soaking in all of the information. Perhaps it was the beginning of his dislike for Judge Parker. Bass, at the time, was not aware of the effect his discussions were having on his son.

Bass knew that the Indian treaties of 1866 provided that the same land was designated for settlement by former slaves of the Indians. But when the Chickasaw legislature on November 9, 1866, passed an Act requesting that the Federal government act in accordance with the treaties, no action was taken. Three years later, delegates of the freedmen petitioned Congress to allow them to move to the designated land, as specified in the agreements. L. N. Robinson, a superintendent of Indian Affairs, wrote that failure to act was a reproach to our boasted civilization and love of justice. In January 1873, the governor of the Chickasaw Nation approved an act allowing 40 acres to each freedman to satisfy the treaty terms. Again, Congress failed to act.[3]

While the question of removing freedmen to the unassigned lands lingered, former slaves from other parts of the country sought entry. A number of organizations were formed to seek migration to the area. One newspaper reported:

The Freedmen's Oklahoma Association has been formed in St. Louis. The association promises every freedman who will go to Oklahoma 160 acres of land free, and it is said too that agents have been sent into the Southern states to start an emigration movement to the Indian Territory among the colored people. The Freedmen's association bases its claim to entry on the lands of the Indian Territory on the treaties of 1866, made by the government with the Creeks and Seminoles.

A leader stated:

We hope to accomplish by the exodus, first and foremost protection. Why, do you know that in the last fifteen years 18,000 Black people have been killed in the south for their political opinion and nothing has been done to remedy the matter? There is no other remedy, so we propose to pull out.[4]

Meanwhile, concern over the possibility of nationwide Black immigration prompted United States Secretary of Interior Samuel Kirkwood to have Commissioner Curtis Holcomb, of the General Land Office, to review the treaties. He reported:

The treaty stipulations, as uniformly understood and construed, have no application to any other freedman than the persons freed from Indian bondage. They relate exclusively to friendly Indians and to Indian freedmen of other tribes in the Indian Territory whom it was the desire of the United States to provide with permanent homes on the lands ceded for that purpose.

Since he did not intend to act in accordance with the treaties, the Commissioner warned prospective settlers:

> *The present attempt to make use of the colored people of the country in the same direction, by deluding them with fictitious assurances that new and congenial homes can be provided for them within this Territory, deserves special reprobation, since its only effect must be to involve innocent people in a criminal conspiracy, and to subject them to disappointment, hardship and suffering.*[5]

As early as 1882, freedmen from other states petitioned Congress to let them settle in the unoccupied lands. On June 16, 1882, Senator Blair of New Hampshire introduced a bill for that purpose. He also wrote Interior Secretary H. M. Teller about the matter. Commissioner of Indian Affairs Hiram Price responded:

> *The most liberal construction that could be placed on these treaty stipulations would not, in my opinion, justify such a scheme or procedure as, the colonization of the colored people from Kansas or other States or the Territories on the Creek and Seminole ceded lands or any other lands in the Indian Territory, and any action inaugurated to carry such a scheme into effect should receive the prompt and unqualified condemnation of this department.*[6]

Two years later, Commissioner Price requested a $25,000 appropriation to enable the Interior Secretary to settle "persons of African descent, and their descendants on the lands mentioned in the 1866 treaties." According to the request, the Secretary sought authorization to assign 160 acres to each head of family,

80 acres to each single person over 21 years of age, and a like amount to each orphan under that age. The Interior Secretary forwarded the request to Congress, and a similar request was also sent to Congress by the President. But no congressional action was taken although the interest of the freedmen continued to be recognized.[7]

In 1886 Commissioner J. C. D. Atkins agreed with his predecessors when he wrote:

> *It has been held by this Department that the language used in both these treaties [the Creek and Seminole treaties of 1866] has reference to freedmen formerly held as slaves by the Indians in Indian Territory or colored persons residing therein at the date of the treaties named, and not to freedmen formerly held in slavery in the Southern States.*[8]

Troubled by the government's failure to act, Bass was also distressed that Judge Parker upheld the Interior Department's position. Even before that decision, Parker had ruled that colored persons who were never held as slaves in the Indian country, but who may have been slaves elsewhere, were like other citizens of the United States. He concluded that such persons had no more rights in the Indian country than other citizens of the United States. He interpreted freedmen in the treaties as those who had been slaves in the Indian Territory and none others. Parker explained that immediately after the abolition of slavery, the government desired to protect the freedmen and considered establishing a Negro colony in the Territory. Though disappointed with Parker's decision, Bass accepted it because of his respect for the judge's integrity. This did not set well with young Ben. The distance between father and son continued to grow as did Ben's resentment of Judge Parker.

Meanwhile, freedmen from other states petitioned Congress to let them settle in the unoccupied lands. For years Texas longhorns on their way to Kansas had grazed on leased land in the district, and in some instances, cattlemen had erected fences and other facilities—actions envied by land-hungry farmers who sought similar privileges. The consensus was that since the Indians had failed to develop the land, their rights should yield to White homesteaders. Several influential factions, including the powerful railroad lobby, pushed to make the land available for homesteading.

By 1878 the railroad companies owned more than ten million dollars worth of property in the Territory by becoming the strongest lobby for opening of the Territory to White settlement. The railroads saw the obvious profit in towns, businesses and agriculture from developing land held by Indians. This led to the amendment of an otherwise routine Indian appropriations bill on March 2, 1889, to open the land for White settlement. Chapman concluded:

> *In the Run on April 22, 1889, and the subsequent commotion over the acquisition of lands, there developed the fixed policy of eliminating the Negroes entirely.*[9]

Because freedmen were denied opportunities to settle in the unassigned lands, Bass saw clearly how the Federal government frustrated their hopes and aspirations. From his many talks with Judge Parker, he knew that President Lincoln had mentioned compensation for 250 years of unrequited toil, and envisioned distributing confiscated and public lands. Others in Washington spoke of forty acres and a mule. Regardless of the proposed reparations, Congress refused to provide homestead land for former slaves. Bass could not have foreseen that the Federal government's action, as well as its inaction during this period, would set the tone for future race relations in the nation, even leading to blatant denials of Constitutional rights for Black citizens.

The lure of the West and *free land, boundless opportunities, a new and better life*, remained primarily for Whites and only minimally for Black Americans. Perhaps out of desperation, some Blacks heeded the call to "Go West" in light of their dismal political, social, and economic plight, particularly in the South. Oklahoma was especially attractive because of its climate, soil and resources. Just as there had been a movement for settlement of the unassigned lands by freed slaves, a similar movement encouraged settlement as American citizens. A pamphlet encouraging such migration, promised the "Colored People of the South":

> *There never was a more favorable time than now for you to secure good homes in a land where you will be free and your rights respected. Oklahoma is now open for settlement. The soil is rich, the climate favorable, water abundant and there is plenty of timber. Make a new start. Give yourselves and children new chances in a new land, where you will be able to think and vote as you please. By settling there you will help open up new avenues of industry, your boys and girls will learn trades and thus be able to do business as other people.*[10]

However, the resistance of southern White immigrants was strong, and racial prejudice undergirded a policy to either eliminate Black settlers or thwart their efforts to settle in the new Territory. One press article claimed:

> *There is an attempt by the Negroes throughout the U.S. to make Oklahoma a Negro state, occupied and governed by Negro people. Agitators are going*

about in different states persuading Negro immigration to Oklahoma.[11]

Because of these racist sentiments, Black pioneers who participated in the land opening fared poorly. In many instances, land that had been claimed but proved unprofitable for farming was sold to Negroes or leased to them as tenant farmers. One newspaper reported:

The Negro in the rush stood but little show and only secured the portions refused by White men as unfit for claiming, a small tract known as the blackjack region. On these lands the Oklahoma Negroes are settled and the entire population does not exceed 1,800 persons. Oklahoma is not a Negro paradise but the happy home of tens of thousands of prosperous White people any report to the contrary notwithstanding.[12]

Bass and most Indians were unaware of President Rutherford Hayes' prediction more than ten years before the land rush of 1889, "that the days of the Indian are drawing to a close." The stark truth of Hayes' prediction haunted the history of the western movement in the Territory. It meant glory and progress for White men and degradation and defeat for the Red and Black man. Indians learned that forever meant until there was a need for the land they occupied. Black people learned that the protection of their rights was optional. Both learned that the will of White people reigned supreme.

CHAPTER **TWELVE**
The Law and the Lawless

Although Bass was not a killer by nature, his job was that of a man hunter. He was fascinated by the hunt which was so unpredictable that it drew on his every skill and sometimes his special intuition. This meant that at times it was necessary to spend days dogging the trail of his quarry, but it could also mean waiting in relative comfort for an outlaw to come to him. This was the method used to apprehend Tom Story.

Being a horse thief was at once a lucrative and despicable profession. Theft of a horse could mean the demise of a farm or a family, so dependent were people on their horses. Generally, some of the best horses in the Southwest were in Indian Territory since almost every Indian had at least one or two excellent mounts. For most Indians, good horses represented tribal wealth. The Territory's horse thieves also coveted them.

Among the noted horse thieves was the well-organized Tom Story gang, which from 1884 to 1889 stole Indian Territory horses and sold them in Texas. Besides Story, the gang had other talented men, all experts in the art of stealing and disposing of horses. Headquartered on the Red River banks in the Chickasaw Nation, the gang in 1889 reversed its operation and stole a herd of horses and mules from George Delaney, who lived in north Texas and sought to sell them in Indian Territory.

Delaney's subsequent investigation revealed Story had stolen his horses and mules and planned to return to Texas in only a few days. He immediately contacted the marshal's office in Paris, Texas, and a warrant was issued for Story's arrest. Bass, who was assigned the warrant, convinced Delaney that, since Story was returning to Texas, they should intercept him as he crossed the Red River. Delaney agreed to accompany Bass as posse. The two men camped close to the Delaware Bend crossing, deep in brush. They fished and even hunted a little while awaiting Story. After four days, they learned from a man crossing the river that Story was expected late the next day. Bass waited in the brush on one side of the trail when Story rode across the ford leading two of Delaney's finest mules.

Bass stepped out of the brush, and challenged the surprised Story, who dropped the lead ropes on the mules. Bass told him he had a warrant for his arrest. Since the lawman still had his gun holstered, Story decided to draw his own.

Bass and Delaney buried the gang leader where he had fallen with a bullet in his chest. With the death of their leader, the Story gang quickly disintegrated, never to be heard from again.

***

Just as he began his career by often concealing his identity, Bass repeated the practice after the Oklahoma Territory was opened for settlement. He was unknown to most of the new inhabitants who surely did not suspect that a Black man could be a Deputy Marshal.

Charles W. Mooney noted that his father (Dr. Jesse Mooney) practiced medicine in both Territories (Indian and Oklahoma). From information taken from his father's diaries, Mooney stated:

> *Dr. Jesse remembered well when Bass Reeves told him about one of his disguises he used in capturing some robbers. In this incident, he dressed as an indigent tenant farmer, with faded and patched overalls, worn out shoes and a greasy creased hat. He drove through the deadly saloon town of Keokuk Falls just inside Oklahoma Territory and adjoining the Creek Nation to the east. The cunning and sagacious officer had received a tip that some outlaws were holed up in an abandoned log cabin about a mile east of Keokuk Falls. Driving a yoke of flea-bitten, aged oxen hitched to a ram-shackled wagon of outdated vintage and usage, he slowly lumbered along, approached the half-hidden cabin in a cluster of trees where smoke wafted slowly from the brick chimney. Driving close to the cabin, he deliberately got the wagon hung on a large tree stump. When the unsuspecting outlaws came out to lift the wagon free so he could be on his way, old Bass calmly reached into his overall pockets and came out with his two big .44 caliber six-shooters and got the drop on the careless outlaws. None challenged his authority after he announced himself to be a Deputy U.S. Marshal. He then disarmed them cautiously, gathering their weapons into the wagon*

and marched all six of them in front of the wagon on foot to the Pottawatomie County jail at Tecumseh, a distance of over 30 miles, arriving about sundown. There they were jailed by Sheriff Billy Trousdale and later taken to the new Federal jail at Guthrie where they were convicted of robbery of the Wewoka Trading Post, then owned by Governor Brown of the Seminole Nation. Dr. Jesse enjoyed telling this fantastic story for many years.[1]

In another case, the trail of a bold killer led Bass to a border town near the Seminole Nation. All he knew was that the gunman was a neatly dressed, handsome young man of medium height with curly blond hair, who always carried a .45 low on his right side in a hand-stitched holster. Bass learned that the outlaw frequented a general store and saloon where he enjoyed playing cards. As usual, Bass knew he would be alerted to the presence of any lawmen in the area.

Dressed as an unarmed, wandering cowboy, the Black lawman casually entered the store and inquired about employment. Moving practically unnoticed by customers, he glanced in the saloon area and recognized the outlaw playing cards. Sizing up the situation, Bass decided to make his move. He ordered a beer and quietly sauntered toward the table where the gunman was seated with his back to the far wall. Walking closely to the right side of the desperado, Bass abruptly placed his badge on the table in front of him and announced he had a warrant for his arrest. Without looking up, the gunman went for his gun, but Bass crashed his beer stein over the man's head and grabbed his gun. While warning others not to interfere, Bass dragged his prisoner out of the saloon, placed him on his horse, and started the long trek back to Muskogee.

***

Selling whiskey was legal in the new Oklahoma Territory. Saloon towns sprang up all along the borders that were next to the Indian Nations. The saloons not only served thirsty travelers and drovers, but also became a gathering place for cattle rustlers, whiskey peddlers, and an assortment of thieves and cutthroats. Knifings, shootings, and gang fights became everyday occurrences. Bass (as noted by Mooney) was one of the first deputies to fearlessly enter the nefarious Corner Saloon alone. It was at the Corner Saloon that more than once he had been called out for a shoot-out by drunken gunslingers who doubted his skill and accuracy with his two six-shooters.

In one shoot-out, Bass was reported to have been wounded, requiring Doctor Mooney's medical attention:*

> *It was late in the summer when a messenger rode up for Dr. Jesse to go to the Corner Saloons on an emergency. The horseback messenger told him, Bass Reeves was shot in the leg and is calling for you. Dr. Jesse quickly saddled his horse, loaded his saddlebags of medicines and instruments, and started on the ten mile ride across the Canadian River into Oklahoma Territory.*
>
> *When the doctor arrived at one of the three Corner Saloons, he found Bass Reeves half-standing and half-sitting on a barroom table. He had been shot in the left leg, above the knee. Still lying on the floor in a pool of blood was a young gunslinger with his drawn pistol still in his hand, dead.*
>
> *"What happened, Bass?" Dr. Jesse asked.*

---

*This is the only account of Bass ever being wounded.

"Just another young gunslinger who doubted my ability with these six guns," the Negro Marshal said. "He was real fast, but like a lot of them, they couldn't shoot both fast and straight," Bass Reeves explained.

The doctor extracted the offending bullet with his tweezer-type probers, then properly medicated and bandaged the gunshot wound. Refusing the usual $3 fee, Dr. Jesse reminded the Marshal of their friendship for eight years and because both had been a friend of Belle Starr, there would be no charge for his services.[2]

Friendship was a highly prized commodity. A friend could save your life, literally. Ned Christie needed a friend badly. Bass Reeves tried to be one.

At war with Federal officers for almost five years, Christie was touted as the most "dreaded of the many desperados who infested that land of outlaws" and the "most dangerous outlaw the marshals had to go after." Christie, a full-blooded Cherokee, was the son of the highly influential Watt Christie. Bass first met father and son during the war when Watt served as a Union volunteer with the Cherokee Home Guard. Both men befriended Bass during his post-Civil War residence in the Cherokee Nation. Ned Christie, the son, an exceptionally intelligent and handsome man, had served with distinction in both houses of the Cherokee legislature. He was an esteemed member of the legislature's Executive Council, which advised Principal Chief Dennis Bushyhead. Like his father, the son was a leading spokesman for Indian rights and longed for the time when Indians would have total self-government throughout the Territory. Indeed, Christie fully expected to help establish such a government.

Christie's conflict with the Federal government began when U.S. Deputy Marshal Dan Maples was shot to death near Tahlequah, capital of the Cherokee Nation. Stories differed as to why Maples was in the area and how Christie was involved. Reportedly, a quarrel he and a companion had with Maples triggered the shooting. Another account indicated that Maples, a recent appointee, was sent to investigate illegal whiskey trading in the area. Because he was unknown, his chances for success were greatly enhanced. He carried a list of suspects and several warrants. Christie, in Tahlequah to attend a special Executive Council meeting, had spent the previous evening drinking with friends. Returning to his boarding house, he was so drunk he passed out in bushes near the shooting scene.

Meanwhile, one of the suspects learned of Maples' presence in the area and decided to kill him. Removing Christie's dark coat, he covered his own light shirt, then lay in wait for Maples. Christie awakened, unaware of the killing but aware that his coat was missing. When it was found, he denied any knowledge of the shooting or that he even had a gun.

But one suspect on Maples' list identified Christie as the man who killed him. Distraught by the accusation, Christie refused to go to Fort Smith to establish his innocence. Bass was aware of the Cherokee's deep resentment over continued injustices against Indians, especially the Federal government's broken promises to them. The two had discussed Congressional action just two years earlier, extending the jurisdiction of Federal courts over offenses committed by Indians. This meant Christie and other Indians would be tried entirely by White judges and juries, still another example of more White control and less Indian self-government. These moves were consistent with other legal loopholes favoring White interests in the Territory. For example, railroads and private persons were free to strip territorial land of valuable timber, since Federal law only covered lands of the United States and Indian lands were not so defined. Tribal courts could try only Indian offenders. Also, Indians could not enforce their tax laws on the White owners of stock grazing in the Territory or levy fines on White men.

Because of the murder charges, Christie's family and friends urged him to surrender and stand trial. Convinced that he could not receive justice in the White man's court, he wrote Judge Parker offering to surrender if he were allowed bond to gain evidence of his innocence. Parker did not respond. Two prominent Indians went to Fort Smith to discuss the matter with him, but in vain. Upon learning a warrant was issued for his arrest, Christie expressed his hatred for all White men, because he felt totally betrayed by the Federal government. Though fluent in English, he vowed never to speak it again. Meanwhile, he was portrayed as a vicious killer, horse thief and armed robber. Indeed, it seemed that every crime in the Territory was blamed on him.

One account claimed:

> *In the safety of the Cherokee Hills he brooded upon his act and the quarrel which preceded the killing and at length he resolved to avenge himself upon all men and especially officers. Collecting a few of his full-blooded [sic] friends whom he could trust, he organized a gang of desperadoes.*
>
> *Eleven murders were credited to Christie. Among his victims were two officers, an Indian woman and a half-breed boy. He was born a killer, cold blooded ruthless; no one knew when or where he would strike next. In the settlement towns, along the isolated paths to the lonely cabins of settlers he stalked relentless in his maniacal [sic] hatred, cool in his knowledge of guns. At one time he had worked as a gunsmith, and his aim was terrifying in its accuracy.*[3]

Another account of Christie's life indicated he had retreated to his farm to live quietly with his family, determined not to go to Fort Smith and be hanged but rather to die at home fighting. Many supporters saw him as a patriot who only fought to protect his family and his freedom. Thus an elaborate system of signals was set up to warn Christie when marshals were in the area. By the time they arrived, he had quietly disappeared into the woods.

Two years after Maples' murder, none of the suspects had been brought to trial because Christie had not been apprehended. In May 1889, a new marshal took over the Parker court. His first order of business was to bring in Ned Christie. The highly regarded Heck Thomas and four other deputies were assigned the task.

Surrounding Christie's home one night, the marshals intended to capture him the following morning. However, at daybreak, barking dogs alerted Christie and the battle began. During the shooting, one of the deputies set a small building afire and the flames reached Christie's cabin. Believing he was killed or had escaped and fearing reinforcements would arrive, the deputies—one seriously wounded—retreated. Actually, Christie was wounded and unconscious when family members and friends rescued him before flames consumed his house.

While recovering from his wounds, he considered his vulnerability. Friends helped him build a new home atop a hill about a half mile from his burnt-out cabin. A virtual fort, it was surrounded by high boulders and dense foliage. For maximum security, the two-story structure was reinforced with double log walls. There were few openings except ten-inch squares for looking out and for placing rifles. Food and ammunition were stocked and water was available from a spring that flowed out of nearby rocks.

Meanwhile Deputy Heck Thomas organized another assault on the fortress, arriving at Christie's hideout on November 12, 1889, with seven other officers. They decided it would take a large regiment of U.S. militia to stand up to Christie and the powerful defense surrounding him. Consequently, Thomas called off the assault.

Soon after Christie was formally charged, Bass had urged his surrender, convinced that his innocence could be proven. He sent word to Christie that he had information that one of the suspects, arrested for whiskey peddling, actually killed Deputy Maples, and requested Christie's cooperation. Bass also believed Christie was an honorable man who, under no circumstances, would shoot a man from ambush. Christie's response, however, was that he wanted nothing to do with Bass or Judge Parker because he could not receive justice in the White man's court and Bass himself was a pawn in the White man's effort to control the Territory.

Despite the failures of other deputies, Bass requested a warrant for Christie's arrest, firmly convinced Christie would not kill him even if given a chance. Bass was familiar with the location of Christie's hideout high in the hills and decided the best approach was from the rear. By setting several green brush fires, he hoped to smoke out the inhabitants and force surrender. In fact, erroneous news accounts reported that Christie had met a violent death. However, one newspaper lamented:

> *U.S. Deputy Marshal Bass Reeves, of Fort Smith, with his posse, made an attack on the house of Ned Christie in the Flint District, who is, perhaps, the most notorious outlaw and desperado in the Indian Territory, and the outlaw's stronghold was burned to the ground. Supposing that the owner had been killed or wounded and was consumed in the building, the news went out that he had met a violent death. But Christie turned up alive, and may cause trouble yet; is said to be on the war path*

fiercer than ever and vows vengeance on the marshal and his posse.

Ned Christie is perhaps the most desperate character in the Territory and there is a large reward offered on his head. He has killed a number of men, among whom might be mentioned the Squirrel brothers, also considered tough men. He is said to be a dead shot, has eluded the officer of the law for about four years and says he will not be taken alive.[4]

Not long after the assault began, Bass knew that Christie had escaped under a screen of smoke, and pursuit would be futile. Now, he was thoroughly convinced that Christie would never be taken alive. The clash between the two was a major news item throughout the Territory. Some newspaper accounts, such as the Muskogee Phoenix, erroneously reported that Bass had been killed by Christie:

Deputy Marshal Bass Reeves was killed Monday by Ned Christie near Tahlequah. Christie is the outlaw wanted for the murder of Dan Maples several years ago. He is one of the toughest characters in the Territory. He has had two cabins burnt by Officers within a few months in a fruitless effort to capture him.[5]

Acknowledging its mistake, the paper later noted that:

The report that Bass Reeves had been killed by Ned Christie in Flint District, Cherokee Nation last week, was without foundation. Bass was 150 miles from the reported place of killing at the time of the alleged killing.[6]

Later, a heavily armed posse of 17 was assigned to bring in Christie. In addition, a 300-pound cannon was shipped by rail from Coffeyville, Kansas, then by wagon over the rocky trail to the fortress site. The posse also brought sticks of dynamite. Taking up positions during the night, they attacked the next morning. More than 2,000 shots were fired and the heavy timbers repelled 38 cannon shots. Frustrated and with several wounded officers, the posse decided the only recourse was to use dynamite. But somehow they had to get close enough to be effective. Under cover of darkness and heavy firing, the lawmen approached the structure and placed sticks of dynamite against the timbers. A long fuse, fired at daybreak, triggered a shattering explosion which blew out a side of the building and started a large fire. Author Bonnie Speer reported:

> *Gold and pink rimmed the eastern horizon as smoke from the burning two-story log cabin swirled across the clearing on the hilltop. Beyond the ravine, the United States deputy marshals, stiff from their long vigil in the cold on this morning of November 4, 1892, tensed as the flames blazed higher into the sky. The roof of the building collapsed and someone shouted in warning. The next instant a tall Indian, almost hidden in the dense cloud of smoke, sped from the burning structure and headed towards the ravine. The deputies shouted for him to halt but he uttered a curse, Damned White marshals, and ran on, his six-shooter blazing. The deputies returned his fire. Their bullets riddled his body and knocked him down. He tried to regain his feet, but another volley settled him. The cool morning breeze lifted the smoke. The deputies stepped out cautiously, unable to believe that the long chase was over, that*

they had finally killed the notorious Cherokee outlaw, Ned Christie.[7]

Sam Maples, embittered son of the slain officer Christie allegedly killed, emptied his revolver into the Indian's dead body. Christie's remains were taken to Fort Smith to be identified. Once in Fort Smith, the reward was claimed, and the body put on public display in front of the Federal jail. A rifle was placed in Christie's dead hands and souvenir photos were taken. Reportedly, this action was requested by a local civic group for the benefit of school children and other sightseers.

The Fort Smith court archives reveal that Ned Christie was only charged with the alleged murder of Deputy Maples and it is not indicated that there was credible evidence he killed Maples. Hence, a reporter concluded:

Ned Christie was declared guilty on circumstantial evidence, and executed for a crime he did not commit.[8]

Similarly, Bass was saddened by the exhibition in Fort Smith. Lamenting the terrible waste of the life of a man who at one time had been a model citizen and an outstanding leader, he believed the true Christie story would never be told.

Many years later the *Daily Oklahoman* (June 9, 1918) reported that a former slave who was adopted by the Cherokees witnessed the Maples killing. Richard Humphrey was a Blacksmith on his way home after a long day's work, when Dan Maples was murdered. Humphrey had not come forward sooner because he feared the Bud Trainor gang. The article reported:

The old Negro, when he saw Trainor take the coat from Christie and with revolver in hand stand behind the stooping tree, knew that there was going to be some desperate deed attempted or committed and as he, with others of the town, was afraid of Trainor, he did not care to be seen walking across the creek on the lower foot log. So he stood and watched and witnessed the assassination.

***

Like Christie, Cherokee Bill became known as "the most fiendish murderer of all those appearing in the annals of the Fort Smith court."

Uncle Ira Franklin of Van Buren told me of Bass' personal relationship with the notorious Cherokee Bill. Bill was born Crawford Goldsby in Fort Concho, Texas. His father, George Goldsby, a soldier in the all-Negro Tenth Cavalry, was a friend of Bass from the time he was stationed at Fort Gibson. Cherokee Bill's mother was named Ellen Beck. Both parents were believed to be of mixed ancestry. When they separated, Ellen cared for Bill's younger brother, Clarence; but Bill was sent to live in Fort Gibson with a Negro lady, Amanda Foster, another of Bass' old friends.

A bright child, Bill attended Indian schools at Cherokee, Kansas (from which his alias was derived), and then the Catholic Indian school in Carlisle, Pennsylvania. When he returned to Fort Gibson, Bill learned of his mother's marriage to William Lynch and of his new stepsister, Maude.

During this period, Bill admired Bass and his dedication to protecting the rights of citizens. Bass, in turn, was impressed with the lad, who was formally educated and displayed leadership promise. Occasionally they discussed the law, Indian rights and self-government.

Bill was quite popular, and one of the boys he knew in the area was Will Rogers, who later gained world-wide fame. Although not considered a bad type, he began to associate with those who were known to drink and fight, including the rough soldiers at the fort.

Obsessed with proving his manliness, Bill learned to imitate the gobble of a wild turkey, a practiced skill among the Indians. The strange, frightening sound was often intended as a fight challenge or death warning to instill fear and gain respect. He seemed filled with rage and, at times, expressed hatred for White people because of racial abuses or possibly because of his stepfather William Lynch, who was reported to be White. In any case, Lynch refused to have anything to do with the boy.

Bill's first serious trouble involved a Black man, Jake Lewis. The two had quarreled at a dance. Bill challenged Lewis to a fistfight and was soundly beaten. Days later, Bill approached Lewis and shot him. When Lewis started to run, Bill shot him again, leaving him for dead. Soon after the shooting, Bass, who was temporarily working out of the Court in Paris, Texas, attempted to locate Bill to dissuade him from further violence. Bass contacted Ike Rogers, a former deputy who often was in his company when covering trails leading out from Keokuk Falls and over to the eastern part of the territory. Bass knew that Rogers was related to Bill's girlfriend, Maggie Glass, and believed Bill would contact her. But Bill, fleeing to the Creek and Seminole Nations, fell in with fellow Cherokees, Bill and Jim Cook, forming the notorious Cook gang. Cherokee Bill became a key member as they robbed stores, banks and railroads, principally in the Cherokee Nation.

The Cooks and most of the other gang members had been cowboys who turned to stealing horses and whiskey peddling, which did not involve much gun play. Cherokee Bill, on the other hand, was fond of gunfire and shot at the slightest provocation. On one occasion, he boarded a train near Fort Gibson and the conductor told him he would have to pay a fare or get off. Bill shot the conductor dead. During a meeting with his stepsister, Maude, at a prearranged location, Bill discovered that her husband, Mose Brown, was present. Thinking that Mose planned to turn him in, Bill shot him seven times with his Winchester.

Several hundred men, including special officers of the railroad and express companies, moved against the Cook gang. Generous rewards were offered for each known gang member, and the Principal Chief of the Cherokees offered $500 for the capture of Bill Cook. He was indeed captured and returned to Fort Smith to face Judge Parker. However, Cherokee Bill remained at large. The crime which led to the end of his violent career was a killing during a store robbery in the town of Lenapah, about 25 miles from Coffeyville, Kansas, where the Dalton gang was finished.

Since the breakup of the Cook gang and now sensing the opportunity to make some easy money, Ike Rogers wanted the reward offered for Cherokee Bill's arrest. There was also the possibility of his reinstatement as a deputy if he could bring Bill in. Rogers had been discharged because it seemed he aided more outlaws than he captured. He, therefore, approached the marshal at Fort Smith with his offer to help. In cooperation with several other deputies, a plan was devised which led to Bill's capture. Rogers invited Bill's girl to his house and got word to Bill that the attractive Maggie would be there. Bill was trapped when he came to visit.

Confined in the Fort Smith jail, Bill made a futile attempt to escape. Tragically, Bill killed a guard using a gun that had been smuggled to him. His warped explanation was, "I didn't want to kill him; I wanted my liberty. Damn a man who won't fight for his liberty. If I hadn't shot him, he would have shot me. If I could have captured the jail, no one would have been killed."[9]

Sentenced by Judge Parker to die on the gallows, Cherokee Bill was defiant to the end. When asked if he had anything to say before his execution, he replied he was there to die, not to make a speech. Then he added, "This is about as good a day to die as any."[10] Judge Parker on the other hand had plenty to say.

Bass, upon returning to the northern area after Bill's death, learned that Cherokee Bill's brother, Clarence, was intent on taking revenge against Ike Rogers. Again, Bass was unable to help avert further violence and killing. Rogers was shot down by Clarence as he stepped from a train in Fort Gibson.

During visits with his mother, Bass expressed his sadness at the needless loss of lives and suffering surrounding Cherokee Bill. It pained him that there was nothing he could do. In a confused mix of responsibility and superstition, Bass saw fit to condemn himself for not doing more. Under the circumstances, he took the number 13 and its relationship to Bill's conviction and sentences as a personal omen. It came to light that:

> *First, Cherokee was believed by some to have killed 13 persons during his career; the offer of $1300 reward affected his capture for killing Earnest Melton; his first sentence to die was pronounced on April 13; he killed Keating on the 26th day of July, or twice 13; Bill was said to have fired 13 shots during the fight with the guards; Judge Parker occupied 13 minutes in charging the jury in the Keating case; the foreman of the jury, boarded at a house numbered 313; the actual hours occupied in the trial numbered 13; the jury was 13 minutes in arriving at a verdict; the jurymen and deputy, who ate and slept together during the trial, made a company of 13; there were 13 witnesses for the prosecution and there were many who believed execution should have followed within 13 minutes after conviction, a total of thirteen 13's.[11]*

***

Throughout his career, Bass had a reputation for being incorruptible, completely immune to the influence of any man when his duty was involved. In one instance, however, he was profoundly influenced. Alice often told the story of her father and Yak-kee, a Creek medicine man.

Bass was on the last leg of a long swing through the Territory, he had reached the North Fork area in the Creek Nation with two wagon loads of prisoners. But he still had one more arrest warrant to serve in North Fork before returning to Fort Smith. Setting up noon camp and leaving his prisoners in the care of his posse, Bass left to arrest Yak-kee, a Creek medicine man.

Reputedly endowed with mystic powers, Yak-kee sold a magic elixir to a potential horse thief that guaranteed to make him invisible if a lawman attempted to arrest him. The potion cost one Indian pony per prescription. Incidentally, two Indians in Bass' group of prisoners had bought the medicine from Yak-kee, and later were arrested as horse thieves.

Meanwhile, Yak-kee allegedly could bewitch anyone who antagonized him. Bass heard reports that he once killed a man whose wife he wanted. She told Bass that Yak-kee witched her husband to death and threatened to kill any of her family members who dared to interfere. She directed Bass to Yak-kee's hut. He was so involved with medicine objects; his arrest was uneventful except for threats to conjure a spell that would kill Bass before they reached Fort Smith. Ignoring the threats, the Deputy Marshal returned to his camp, loaded Yak-kee into a wagon with his other prisoners, and headed to Fort Smith.

By nightfall, Bass felt very stiff and sore despite having felt well all day. The next morning he resumed the Fort Smith trip. Bass recalled:

Although I rode a good saddle horse I was unable to keep within sight of the wagons. When I reached their camp at noon they were done eating and the prisoners, shackled together, were lying under the trees asleep. With the greatest difficulty I dismounted, and fell forward against a tree, aching in every limb, and my eyes were so swollen that I could scarcely see. I could eat nothing and seemed possessed of a consuming thirst. My knees refused to bear the weight of my body, and feeling that my last hour had come I thought to take a last look upon the man whom I felt was responsible for my present condition. He was lying on his back asleep, and his coat had turned partly over so that a concealed inner pocket was brought into view. I saw a string dangling from it and made up my mind that it was attached to his 'conjur-bag.' Gently I dragged myself to his side and with a jerk drew from his pocket a mole-skin bag, filled with bits of roots, pebbles and tiny rolls of short hair, tied with blue and red strings. I tossed it as far as I could, and saw it float away on the bosom of a creek that flowed alongside the camp. With a start Yak-kee awoke.

'Reeves,' said he, 'you stole my conjur-bag.'

'Yes, I did,' I said, 'and it is now sailing down the creek.' The old man promised all kinds of pay if I would return it, but I feared it less as it sailed down the creek than when it was in the hands of Yak-kee.

'I can't conjur any more,' said the old man; 'my power is gone. Take off this chain and I will follow

you like a dog.' I declined to do this, however, and the prisoners started on. From the moment the bag touched the water I began to feel relieved. I later mounted my horse and when I caught up with the party in the evening I felt as well as ever. Yak-kee told me afterward that if he had not lost his 'conjur-bag', I would have been dead before they reached Fort Smith; I believe it, too."[12]

Bass' reputation for enforcing the law and helping those in need was known far and wide. His name was probably used to threaten criminals and would be criminals alike. In September 1892, a battered woman, Mattie Bittle, wrote Bass about her abusive husband, George. She wrote:

I wish he hade stade in the penitintry he got a stick and beat me. I don't think I can get over it.

Before Bass could act, Mattie died of her injuries and Bittle was arrested for her murder.[13]

Bass did, however, manage to bring in To-sa-Lo-Nah, alias Greenleaf—the first time he had been arrested although he had been an outlaw for 18 years. To-sa-Lo-Nah was considered extremely dangerous. He had killed seven men, four of whom had assisted deputies in hunting him. The last one, named Barma Maha, he first shot down and then put twenty-four bullets in his body. "Every marshal that has ridden in Seminole, Creek and Chickasaw country has carried writs for him (Greenleaf). But, for some time past it has been impossible for an officer to get any one to assist in hunting him as it was almost sure death to do so unless the hunt was successful." When Bass finally captured To-sa-Lo-Nah, "people who had known him long doubted it and flocked to see if it was really so, some riding as far as eighteen miles to convince themselves of his identity."

Court records show that Bass had originally sworn out a warrant for Greenleaf and Maha's arrest nearly ten years before; but, during the interim, a violent quarrel erupted between the two that led to the killing of Maha.[14]

CHAPTER **THIRTEEN**
Father and Son

The children were growing. In a few short years, Alice would be off to school. Jinney's plans for her daughter were on track. Alice was going to be a teacher. Jinney hoped that Alice would be able to go to school in Langston, Oklahoma. The Negro citizens of Langston had petitioned the Oklahoma Industrial School and College Commission in July 1892 for a college for Negroes.

Alice remained a quiet child. She was a comfort to both her mother and her father. On the other hand, Ben had proven to be a handful. The relationship between Bass and Ben was strained to say the least; though Ben, to his father's delight wanted to be a lawyer. When he was old enough, through Judge Parker's

Assistance, Ben took odd jobs around the Fort Smith courthouse so that he could get a feel for and gain experience with the law. However, one day he suddenly announced that he would never become a lawyer. Angrily declaring contempt for the White man's law, Ben claimed it was made by and intended only to protect White men, reminding Bass that he had been wrongfully charged by White men and White men were the only ones who sat on juries. To the son, his father's life dramatized a malaise footnoted almost daily by events in the Territory.

Resentful over Bass' admiration for Parker, Ben accused the judge of exploiting his father from the very beginning of their relationship.

Ben claimed that Parker, while expecting his deputy marshal to risk his life upholding the law, knew that neither his father nor any other Black or Red man shared legal protections equally with White men. Ben also charged that Parker's frequent show of religious piety and sense of justice was based solely on vengeance with no concern for Christian understanding or compassion. Though sharply stung by his son's rebuke, Bass avoided argument. Instead, he wanted each of his children to decide independently what was right and how far each would go to defend their own beliefs. Ben resented his father's long absences and openly criticized him for spending all of his time tending other people's problems and ignoring everything except wearing a badge and being a marshal. Behind his father's back, Ben also spoke disparagingly of his father's crude manner of speech.

Bass saw his son's outbursts as sure signs of trouble ahead. To make matters worse, Ben was seeing a woman whom Bass thought totally unsuitable for his son. He and Jinney agreed that Ben had been adversely influenced by Cassie, a mixed-race, Muskogee beauty who sometimes visited relatives at Fort Smith. Their son had spent most of his spare time in her company, listening intently to her sharp criticisms of existing racial injustices. While Jinney accepted the relationship, Bass had reservations about Ben's girlfriend, especially since he believed she looked down on him.

When Bass returned from an extended trip, Jinney broke the news to Bass. Ben and Cassie were engaged. Though feeling he had been completely ignored, his resentment was tinged with remorse. After all, who could he blame for not being home more often? And he could not expect to be included in everything that occurred while he was away—although Bass and Jinney agreed that neither Ben nor Cassie were ready for marriage. Indeed, Bass had investigated Cassie's past. The information that he received from his sources in Muskogee convinced him that Cassie was a flirt. This assessment coincided with his personal judgement of her. Bass felt that her clothes fit too tightly and that she wore too much jewelry. Besides, he thought his son's self-centered nature would prevent him from being a responsible husband and father.

Before Ben and Cassie could marry, tragedy struck. On March 19, 1896, Jinney died of cancer. Though plagued with illness for some time, her condition had not been considered serious. The years of worry over Bass' safety no doubt affected her health. Particularly stressful was Ben's relationship with Cassie. Jinney loved Ben and Alice equally, but practically doted on Ben. Enmeshed in Territory matters, Bass' attention was directed from Jinney and the problems at home. Since she rarely complained and refused to see a doctor, it was difficult to know how much she suffered. When her noticeable loss of weight and energy became obvious, it was too late for medical attention.

Bass was devastated. Jinney had always been there to greet him when he returned from his many trips to the Territory. She had remained an attractive woman over the years and Bass always looked forward to seeing her. Jinney had loved living on the farm in Van Buren and, although deeply understanding, she could not reconcile her fears in regards to Bass' dangerous work. Naturally reserved, she dreaded the pervasive violence in the Territory. She found comfort in the surroundings of Van Buren, but looked forward to the day they could return to the Nations. Typically, home and church were foremost in her life. Unlike Bass and Paralee, she was not an organizer of their church in Van Buren, but had become a devoted member and remained so for life. While growing beautiful flowers and tending her own small vegetable garden, Jinney's life had been centered on her children.

Bass took Jinney's death very hard and became extremely depressed and wracked with guilt. He felt that he should have spent more time with his family. Unfortunately, another blow was about to befall Bass. The winds of change were sweeping through and wreaking havoc on Fort Smith and the man Bass had admired for many years.

Step by step, Congress had continued the process of dismantling the Parker court. Finally in 1895, Congress set the Date of September 1, 1896, when the Fort Smith Court's jurisdiction over the Indian Territory would come to an end. Judge Parker, although 58 years old, looked much older. The strain over the past 21 years had left a telling mark.

> *Yet he presided with the same ease and dignity that has characterized his deliberations all these years. His kindly face belies the many hard things that have been said of him, and he is the same counselor and friend to the wayward that he has always been.*[1]

But Parker's health began to decline. The law was his life and the Fort Smith court was his life blood. Losing his authority over the Territory was like a death knell. On July 9, 1896, it was reported that he was too sick to hold court. His deteriorating condition was attributed to his enormous work load for the past 21 years. Twelve thousand four hundred ninety cases had been docketed involving persons charged with violating every Federal statute in the books. Of this total, 9,454 had been convicted by jury trial or entered guilty pleas. Court was held for 10-12 hours and sometimes longer each day, six days a week, term after term. His work had taken its toll.

In early September, the *St Louis Republic* sent a reporter to interview Judge Parker as he approached the end of his jurisdiction over the Territory. Reporter Ada Patterson had dreaded the meeting, having been told of the Judge's harsh nature. Following the interview conducted in Parker's home, Ada Patterson wrote her opinion of the Judge in the following words:

> *He is the gentlest of men, this alleged sternest of judges. He is courtly of manner and kind of voice and face, the man who has passed the death sentence on more criminals than has any other judge in the land. The features that have been in them the horror of the Medusa to desperadoes are benevolent to all other human kind. He spoke on his personal views of crime and law enforcement with such feeling that he sat up from his pillows ... and the weak voice grew strong.*[2]

The reporter went on to quote a prominent member of the Fort Smith bar:

> *Judge Parker is learned in the law; is contentious of the administration of it. He has a kind heart and a big soul. He is absolutely faithful to his home ties. All I could say of him for days would be summed up thus: He is a good man.*[3]

Judge Parker died several months later on November 1. Isaac C. Parker was not only viewed by many as the greatest judge in the history of the West, he was referred to in the massive legal treatise, *Greenleaf on Evidence,* as one of the greatest American trial judges. Following his death, the *Fort Smith Elevator* of November 20, 1896, observed:

> *American civilization has produced a multiplicity of characters, but only one Parker. It is impossible to even imagine what the record of the Territory might have been had not the strong arm of Judge Parker extended over it.*

Bass was the only deputy known to have served throughout the jurist's tenure (1875-1896) and on to statehood. Next to the early discipline and training Bass had received from his mother, Judge Parker had shaped his life. His courage and unselfish devotion to protecting human life and respecting the rule of law sparked Bass' career. Bass seriously considered resigning after Judge Parker's death. However, Bass did not quit despite his disappointment with the Federal government's failure to enforce the law for the protection of all citizens.

After Judge Parker's death and since his Court's jurisdiction was transferred to a new court in Muskogee, Bass also relocated. The move of approximately 60 miles was not a problem, since it brought him closer to his work and the homes of Ben and Alice. He had always considered his children the greatest of his blessings and was proud each had received formal education. Alice was one of the first students to attend the Langston Colored Agricultural and Normal University. Langston, established in 1897, was the first institution of higher learning for Black students in the territories. She later taught school in Muskogee for many years. Alice greatly admired her father for the adversity he had known and for what he had accomplished with his life. She was familiar with his career and spoke proudly of his accomplishments, which she was pleased to share with me.

Always interested in education for young people, Bass provided Dora, his sister Jane's daughter, with an education. She too, became a teacher like Alice. Alice used to tell the story of her father traveling across the countryside. He was known to ride up to a schoolhouse window, sit quietly in the saddle, and listen to the teacher. In cold weather, he would enter the school, squeeze his long legs under a desk, rub his mustache, and try to appear comfortable. Education, book learning, would always remain just beyond his grasp.

CHAPTER **FOURTEEN**
Devotion to Duty

He sat tall and straight astride the big sorrel gelding, his upper lip hidden behind a fox tail mustache, long arms and huge hands accentuating broad shoulders and a lean muscular V-torso. Bass Reeves rode slowly down Muskogee's dusty main street in Indian territory. As he veered toward the hitch rail fronting the U. S. Marshal's Office, he could have been mistaken for a professional gunfighter except for the glistening star pinned high on his chest.

For nearly 25 years, Bass Reeves had been a U.S. Deputy Marshal in the two crime-ridden Indian territories. Two days earlier, he had narrowly survived an ambush by three outlaws he had doggedly pursued, seriously wounding one and forcing a meek surrender of the other two. He had delivered them to the jail and was about to report to newly-appointed Marshal Leo Bennett, a former Indian agent and Bass' longtime friend. Dismounting, the Deputy Marshal looped his sorrel's reins around the hitch rail as Toby, his companion, a large black dog, quietly settled underneath. It had been a long journey for Bass from deep in the Creek Nation. Bone-tired, he yearned for a few days' rest and rehabilitation with his family. But that was not to be. Events had occurred in his absence that would change his life forever.

His son Ben had become increasingly jealous soon after his marriage to Cassie. His wife seemed intent on attracting male admirers and having a good time. As a railroad worker, Ben traveled frequently. During his absence, he suspected that Cassie was seeing Jimmy Long, an unemployed "fancy Dan" gambler who wore expensive clothes and spent money freely. He was rumored to be part of a horse-stealing ring, but no charges were ever brought against him. Before her marriage, Long had showered Cassie with so much attention, her family discouraged the relationship and forbade her from seeing him. Long had been one of the reasons she visited Fort Smith when she met Ben. Later, when he questioned Cassie about his suspicions, she denied any involvement with Long.

However, when Ben returned home from an overnight run, he learned that Cassie was visiting at a friend's house. He was also informed that Long was there. Although unskilled in gunmanship, he stuck an old pistol in his belt and went to confront Long. At first Long hid, but then appeared and admitted to Ben that he was romantically involved with his Cassie and planned to go to Kansas with her. If Ben did not like it, Long added, he could get a gun and the matter would be settled one way or the other. Whereupon Ben opened his coat and drew. As the two men exchanged shots, Cassie somehow got caught in the crossfire and was slain. Whether she intended to run away with Long was never determined. Long fled. Ben, who had been wounded in the gunfight, immediately turned himself in. During subsequent treatment for a head wound, Ben, with an apparent change of heart, seized the opportunity to escape.

During Bass' absence, Marshal Bennett had been uncertain about what to do with an arrest warrant he held. Reluctant to assign any other deputy to the case, he also had grave misgivings about expecting Reeves or any other man to trail and capture his own son—charged with the murder of his wife. Usually composed, the Bass was visibly shaken as he paced the floor in the marshal's office, reflecting on how clearly defined the law had always been. His only concern had been to enforce it vigorously. But the law that he revered was now confounding and clashing with his love for his son. Finally, he told Marshal Bennett that since it was his son who was sought, he preferred to make the arrest himself. Bennett could not deny Bass' request for the writ. Besides, both men knew the father was more able to anticipate the movements of his son. An article appearing in the *Muskogee Daily Phoenix* later described the scene:

> *With a devotion of duty equal to that of the old Roman Brutus, whose greatest claim to fame was that the love for his son could not sway him from justice, he said, Give me the writ.*[1]

None of the past seemed to matter as Marshal Bennett reluctantly handed Bass the warrant for Ben's arrest. Leaving the office, Bass hastily gathered supplies and an extra horse for the extraordinary journey ahead. Ben was last seen heading south on his favorite horse with at least a one-day head start. Bass believed he would catch up in due time with Toby's expert help.

There were too many tracks on the main road out of Muskogee to pick up a single trail. Stopping at a settlement about ten miles south, Bass learned that a young man on a Palomino horse had passed through almost two days before. He had veered off the main road to the left and was moving fast. Knowing the stride and the kind of shoes Ben's horse wore, Bass was soon following the tracks of a single horse. He knew that they were heading southeast toward the Cookson hills, then into the Sans Bois mountains and across its valleys to the Kiamichi range. The Deputy Marshal also speculated that Ben's pretty Palomino was more suited for show than riding in rough backcountry. In short, the fugitive son could not possibly cover the same distance as fast as his more savvy father.

Surmising that Ben was headed for Mexico, Bass calculated that at some point he would begin to move in a westerly direction. The Deputy Marshal called a reluctant Toby off the trail, then used cattle paths and small trails as short cuts to intercept Ben's trail when he emerged from the rugged mountain country. Picking up the Palomino's scent coming out of some woods, Toby again found the trail leading across the Red River into northeast Texas.

Thoughts of the strange circumstances flooded Bass' mind. As a fugitive he had escaped from Texas to the Indian Territory seeking refuge; and now his son, as a fugitive, was escaping from the same territory to Texas seeking refuge. Bass also recalled that as a youngster Ben had been fascinated by the story that possibly his grandfather Arthur had headed to Mexico many years ago. On several occasions, he spoke of visiting that country and now it appeared he would use this opportunity.

They were in open land now and Ben was not far ahead. Growing more apprehensive, Bass began to think of their meeting. Would Ben give up easily, or would he give up at all? Each night he looked for a fire. He was sure Ben didn't know that when on the scout, a fire was taboo since it could pinpoint one's location. Late one evening, he saw a fire in the distance about where Ben would camp for the night. Before sun-up the next morning, he and Toby came upon Ben, who was still asleep. When awakened, Ben, unarmed, seemed relieved and told Bass he knew he was not far behind him.

Trail-weary and haggard, Ben expressed extreme remorse, particularly for the disgrace he had brought to the family, the main reason he decided to escape. To his father, he seemed a frightened little boy caught misbehaving. He felt ashamed that he brought leg irons with him. They soon broke camp in search of the nearest town and a hearty meal.

***

The return was extremely difficult both for hunter and hunted. Repeatedly, Ben told his father that he had not intended to shoot his wife, Cassie, it was all a terrible mistake for which he would have to pay. Occasionally, they talked openly about each other and their family, but they spent much of the time in silence.

As a favor to Bass, officials encouraged Ben to plead guilty to a lesser charge based on the ambiguous circumstances of Cassie's death. However, because Ben refused to cooperate with defense efforts and insisted that his father not attempt to intercede on his behalf, he was found guilty of murder and sentenced to life in the federal prison at Fort Leavenworth, Kansas. Ben served nearly 12 years of the sentence and was released.

Reflecting on his years serving in Judge Parker's court, Bass realized the high price it had cost his family. He was sure Jinney's worry and concern over his welfare had contributed to her illness. He also felt partially responsible for Ben's conduct and felt that, if they had spent more time together, perhaps the tragedy could have been averted. Since Ben tended to avoid confrontation and violence, he was ill prepared for a shoot-out. But somehow he felt he must resort to his father's method of resolving disputes by the gun. Filled with a strong sense of guilt, Bass also thought that, if he had spent more time with the Goldsby Boy or got to Ned Christie, lives may have been spared. Indeed remorse for actions taken and not taken filled his mind. His feelings may have been fueled by the deep hurt that one of the youngsters he had opened his home to was later convicted of rape and sentenced to prison. Bass had been instrumental in arranging for the lad to work for Judge Parker. The boy had assaulted a young lady who also worked in the Parker home.

Since the past was past and there was nothing he could do to change it, Bass looked forward to his more frequent visits with his family in Van Buren. This led to renewing a close relationship with his sister's son William Luck Brady.

During his sojourns in Van Buren, Bass spent considerable time fishing with the boy and visiting with his mother. Bass loved to hear Luck and Paralee sing together as they both had outstanding voices.

For Dad, a highlight of this period was attending Judge Parker's court when Uncle Bass testified. He had heard many stories about this huge man with the long gray hair and beard and he knew how much Uncle Bass admired him. But Dad was not prepared for the impressive scene of highly polished wooden columns, tables and benches, and of course, the array of characters. He would never forget, however, the man who was in charge of the people and the event, with the large gold chain draped across his very wide vest. Nor would he forget the respect and obvious affection shown Uncle Bass by this all-powerful man.

Awed by stories related by his older brother, Johnny, Luck yearned to be part of his uncle's law work. Persistence eventually paid off. While in his early teens, Luck was allowed to accompany his uncle into the Territory. Always remaining in camp, he helped the cook, cared for the horses and performed other chores about the camp. Most of the time, Bass' dog was left with him, providing great company and a guard for the prisoners. They were aware he would attack them at the slightest provocation.

Beginning with his first trip, Luck noted a changed Uncle Bass who hardly laughed or showed his lighthearted side. Seldom speaking to the other men, he constantly chatted with his dog and horse. Always alert to everything going on, he even moved about at night, often leaving camp before sun-up. In the evenings when they were camped or riding the trail, they talked of many things but mostly of Bass' years as a deputy. It was clear he had given considerable thought to his life and work but never spoke favorably or unfavorably about Luck becoming a lawman.

Bass often returned to the subject of killing as part of his job. He was quick to point out that those who made a conscious decision to kill usually gave lawmen no choice but to kill. From experience, Bass learned not to trust most men. The uncle advised the nephew to rely on himself and trust in God, to strive to become a good and honorable man who always kept his word once it was given. For himself, he expressed pride in having carried out the oath he gave Judge Parker many years before. At no time did Luck hear his uncle express any disappointment or frustration that the law he so faithfully served had grievously failed him.

CHAPTER **FIFTEEN**
Above The Law

The end of Reconstruction in the South ushered in a new wave of racial discrimination across the nation, especially within the new Oklahoma Territory created by Congress in May 1890. Nothing in Bass' experience had prepared him for the blatant racism that flared despite the so-called Organic Act, which specifically required the new territorial government to make no distinction in civil or political rights because of race or color. President Benjamin Harrison, who opened the Oklahoma District to settlement, was aware of mounting racial problems and met with a Black delegation in 1890 regarding its concerns. He seemed favorably impressed as the group's spokesman explained:

We desire to get away from the associations that cluster about us in the Southern states. We wish to remove from the disgraceful surroundings that so degrade my people, and in the new territory in Oklahoma, show the people of the United States and of the world that we are not only loyal citizens but that we are capable of advancement.[1]

The President replied that the community, which denied to a portion of its members their rights under the law, severed the only safe bond of social order and prosperity. Because of his appointive power, the President had considerable influence in the Oklahoma Territory. His appointees were bound by oath to protect the Constitutional rights of all persons regardless of color. In the summer of 1890, George Steele, the first territorial governor, appointed a Negro treasurer of Logan County. The following year, a Black man was appointed county clerk. These appointments increased White resistance and hostility. A Daily Oklahoman editorial declared:

We hereby declare for white supremacy in Logan County. We believe that it is to the best interest of Logan County that white men be placed in public offices, and that all deputyships be given to white men.

The next year the editor of the *Guthrie Daily Leader*, a member of the Territorial Assembly, introduced a bill to eliminate Black citizens as office holders. Later, the Oklahoma City *Weekly Times-Journal* observed:

... it is preposterous for any one to make a fuss over the dangers of Negro domination in a state where there are ten White men to each Negro.[2]

Despite numerous appeals by Black citizens for public officials to enforce the law, violence and lawlessness continued unabated. In 1901, the *Oklahoma Guide* asked: "What is the Matter with Governor Jenkins?" The editorial questioned why the governor had failed to act when racial violence occurred within 43 miles of his office. His officials failed to protect the basic rights of Black citizens. The *Indian Chieftain* (August 29, 1901), reported that Major H. C. Miller issued a proclamation to the citizens of Sapulpa urging that if they are determined to rid the town of the Negro population, let them do so in a peaceful law-abiding manner. The article also noted that mob violence also spread to Stroud in the Oklahoma territory. Reports were that:

> *A mob of gamblers and toughs organized last night and ran all Negroes out of town. Two houses, in which Negroes lived, were torn down. The contents of the building were burned. The trouble started when a Negro drew a revolver on a white man.*

In the spring of 1902, Governor Thompson Ferguson was notified that private proclamations had been posted at Lawton (Comanche County) warning all Negroes to leave town.[3] The same date, Black citizens appealed to Heck Thomas, Police Chief of Lawton. Thomas, a former Georgian and deputy for Parker, was a much-celebrated lawman. As a young Atlanta police officer, Thomas was acclaimed for his role in quelling a Negro mob. It was reported that Thomas came to Lawton "with a reputation like few other lawmen of his time. He kept terrorism by gangs at a minimum. Gunslingers feared him."[4] Apparently, enforcement of the law regarding Negro rights had a different meaning for him. Heck Thomas reportedly told Negro citizens they had to go, "and don't stand on the order of going but go at once."[5] No Negro could enter Greer County, an area of about 1,400,000 acres, according to the unwritten law. (The original opening in 1889 consisted of 2,000,000 acres.) Press reports of a mob uprising in Shawnee, Greer County, stated:

The colored population of the city suffered the brutal assaults of a crowd of whites of the lower class, who, when daylight comes, hide away. The damage done was sustained wholly by the colored element, who in the majority of cases were unprepared to protect themselves. A Negro woman and a Negro man were shot by the mob, the latter being in a serious condition and several more Negro men were ... beaten up.[6]

Reportedly, 600 Negroes had filed claims in the new country and nearly everyone was driven away from his claim or forced to sell it, in most cases for a mere pittance (Oklahoma Guide, April 16, 1906) Two months before Judge Parker's death, the press noted:

Whitecappers are expelling negroes from the southern part of this territory. Not a colored resident remains in Norman. Last night eight whitecappers whipped an old Lincoln County negro and his two sons and ordered the three out of the county. The same aggregation of whitecappers, numbering about a dozen, warned a white man named Scott with many negro tenants that all the latter must leave. The same work is going on extensively.[7]

Mob activity continued even though Governor Barnes claimed in 1896 that no mob violence had appeared in the Oklahoma Territory. He explained that this indicated the lawful tendency of the people who tilled the soil and cared for livestock. "They performed the tasks necessary to growth of towns and the transportation of goods." (*Indian Chieftain*, September 24, 1896) Clearly, the governor overlooked the dire experiences of Black citizens who attempted to settle in the new territory. Popular history again picks up the same theme and fails to provide an accurate account of this history. Overlooked are the tragic experiences of Black citizens who attempted to settle in the new territory. *The Federal Courts of the Tenth Circuit, A History*, states:

> *After the first explosion of land disputes subsided, crime actually declined. Roving gangs of outlaws as had plagued Indian Territory for over a generation were rare. The territory was settled mainly by young families from midwestern farm country where respect for law was an overriding element in their upbringing.*

The wave of lawlessness and racial violence soon reached the Indian Territory and Bass Reeves. The *Muskogee Phoenix* reported:

> *Ed Chalmers, a state-raised Negro, was living in a little hut not far from Wybark with a white woman by the name of Mary Headley. They were to be married and certainly claimed to their neighbors that they were man and wife. So far as is known they were both harmless and peaceable residents and were industrious farmers. The fact that a white woman and a Negro man were married and were living as man and wife grated on the nerves of some of the residents of this section.*
>
> *A few of the near residents, all supposed to be white persons, assembled Saturday night and during the rain and storm proceeded to the humble home ...*

and literally murdered them in cold blood ... The white woman was shot to death in her bed and her Negro consort was shot all to pieces, though he lived until nine o'clock Sunday morning ... Before he died ... he made a dying statement in which he named several parties as the guilty ones.

Early Sunday morning a messenger came running into Muskogee and informed the officers that a man and woman had been killed across the river. Deputy Bass Reeves was at once dispatched to the scene of the triple tragedy ... and instructed to find out all the facts as far as possible.[8]

Bass made several arrests for the murders, but there is no written record of the cases ever coming to trial. He had previously befriended young Chalmers and taken a personal interest in his life. In 1901, at Sapulpa in the Creek Nation, a white mob ordered all Negroes to leave the area. Those who refused were driven from their homes. The next year, a race riot broke out at Braggs, near Muskogee. Several White men had horsewhipped a Negro and, when his friends sought revenge, a fight ensued. One White and five Negroes were seriously wounded. Bass was sent to the scene where he and another deputy arrested twenty-four men who were charged with taking part in the race war and bound over for trial. Generally, lawmen serving in Judge Parker's former jurisdiction lived up to their responsibilities despite the strong racial sentiments of many newly-arrived settlers.

In the Indian Territory town of Holdenville during 1904, local newspapers reported a dispute over use of a local hotel:

The trouble has reached that stage that Marshal Bennett has sent one of his best men there and the attorney for the district has been sent to the spot to settle the trouble if possible. Holdenville is a white town. It is in the heart of a country where the colored population is dense. Negroes were not allowed to remain overnight and merchants began to suffer a loss of trade. So they resolved to change things and a number of them backed up a proposition to establish a hotel for Negroes. The house was started and a few nights later it was raided by irate whites who are opposed to Negroes, and all the furniture was thrown into the streets. A number of the leading men have asked the officers here to interfere and they left for Holdenville this afternoon. Holdenville has 2,000 people but no Negroes.[9]

Bass was one of the officers who made arrests. Later, he was pleased that United States Attorney William Mellette publicly stated that Holdenville citizens could not run Negroes out of town or keep them from coming there. Mellette was also commended by the Black press:

The stand taken by the U.S. Attorney, Honorable Wm. Mellette in the Holdenville affair, and his support by the balance of the court officials, is commendable and shows that the officials in this Western District from Judge to constable, are in favor of enforcing the law and are in favor of justice and right.[10]

Bass had dealt with desperadoes who insisted on freedom and personal liberty without assuming any sense of community responsibility. Now he was confronted with settlers who, while seeking freedom and personal liberty, ignored their civic responsibilities and basic respect for the law. Those who forcibly deprived others of their rights and property were no different from the other desperate characters and outlaws Bass had known. He had often heard Judge Parker speak of citizens' relationship to the law, that "none are so high in station as to be above it, and none so low as to be beyond it. Those who allow themselves to degenerate into a mob become criminals themselves." (Charge to Grand Jury, August, 5,1895) The battle up to this time had been establishing the supremacy of the law over the lawless. Now the fight was being waged over color, establishing the supremacy of White citizens over Black citizens by mob rule. Bass would often talk about Judge Parker's strong feelings on the subject: He remembered the judge saying:

The law must be vindicated ... if this great government is to teach to the people the high object lesson that they can depend on its courts and thus secure protection to life and destroy that hideous monster which now curses the country called the mob. You say to a community that as sure as a crime is committed, so sure will the party who has committed it be brought to merited justice, as the law prescribed that punishment, and you won't find any mobs in that community.

During the twenty years of Judge Parker's jurisdiction, there had been only three cases of mob lynching. (During a five-year period between 1890 to 1895, there were 1,118 lynchings in the United States.)

As other Black deputies were appointed in the territory, strong feelings of racial prejudice began to surface. After Deputy Lee Thompson's gun discharged during an off-duty incident, the Fort Smith Elevator reported December 8, 1893, that this was:

The second one of Mr. [Marshal] Crump's negro deputies who have succeeded in getting mixed up with the minions of the law during the past month or so. At the present rate it is to be hoped that the whole batch of negro marshals will either be in jail or disposed of in some other way.

The same newspaper on August 2, 1895, commented:

Negro deputy marshals are obnoxious in the extreme to the good people of the Indian Territory, and there is seldom one found who is fit to be appointed to such a position, yet by some means Marshal Crump finds it necessary to employ them, much to the dissatisfaction of the people over whom his court has jurisdiction.

Bass sorely missed Judge Parker's deep respect for the lawman's work and the special problems he faced. On every assignment, a deputy's life was on the line and death was his ever-present companion. The judge allowed no interference with the work of the deputies as long as their conduct and methods were legal. Now strong efforts were made to restrict the enforcement authority of Black lawmen. In July 1901, Jack Walter, a Black deputy working out of the Ardmore court, arrested a White man. Some of the leading citizens of Pauls Valley swore out a warrant for Walter's arrest charging him with disturbing the peace. Later, at a town meeting, resolutions were adopted protesting the hiring of Black marshals and asked that Walter be fired. The marshal in charge of the district refused to do so. Several days later, a local news-paper reflected the racial bias:

The action of Negro deputy, Jack Walter, at Pauls Valley a few days ago has justly called forth the censure and condemnation of the people of that city upon his head, upon Captain Jno. S. Hammer, who appointed him, and upon Office Deputy A. M. Foss, whose encouragement he received.

When Negroes are appointed as United States Deputy Marshals with full power to arrest white people it is indeed high time to call a halt.

The white citizens of the Southern District have no objections to Negro deputies appointed so long as they arrest only men of their color, but when swaggering Negroes armed with Winchesters and vested with authority to arrest, so far overstep the people's customs as to attempt to arrest a white man ... it is time for the installation of new public officials who have the interest of the people at heart.

Yet the Negro was not as much to blame as was his supervisors who have stood by him even to the extent of endorsing what he had done.

The citizens of Pauls Valley did right in condemning such contemptible and unwarranted conduct by the Negro and in censuring Marshal Hammer for allowing a Negro the privileges which he exercised. (Ardmore Appeal)

While Bass' reputation had been widely known and his authority never challenged or limited, most of the newly arrived settlers in the territory had difficulty accepting this bold and assertive Black man. One man, who sought work as a posse-man and guard, refused to go with Bass, "Because he was a Negro and I didn't think a White man should work under a Negro." (William's, Indian Pioneer Papers) *Nobody works for a nigger,* became a common expression. Associated with this view was the attitude, shared by many, that Reeves did not want to get mixed up with White people, saying in effect that only White men should do White men's business.

Another recent settler, without any basis whatsoever, stated, "he [Reeves] didn't bother much with White outlaws but worked after the Creek and Cherokee Negroes and Indians." (William's, Indian Papers) Most newcomers, while projecting their own racist notions, were obviously unaware of Bass' reputation. Many had no knowledge of the years Bass spent arresting outlaws of every color and stripe throughout the Territory while working out of the courts in Fort Smith; Paris, Texas; Wetumka, and Muskogee Indian Territory. Nor would they understand that he served as lead deputy marshal for the Creek, Seminole, and Chickasaw nations. Newspapers contained more racial distinctions and pointed out Bass' experience in arresting Black and Indian fugitives. He is quoted as saying:

> *Seminole Indian is the hardest man to arrest of any class of people he ever met; that he is always ready, and if given a ghost of a chance he will shoot you and run. (The Chickasaw Enterprise, November 28, 1901)*

> *... The old deputy says the worst criminals and the hardest to catch are the Seminole Indians and Negroes. They stick together better, fight quicker*

and fight to kill. (Oklahoma Times-Journal, March 8, 1907)

***

While the concept of White supremacy was taking hold, concerted efforts were underway to minimize Bass' accomplishments and discredit him. Not surprisingly, stories were written which quoted him as saying that as a slave he accompanied his master into battle during the Civil War. One deputy marshal later wrote that Bass told him he served his master in the war as a body servant. Bass vehemently denied these stories and was particularly offended because of his abhorrence of any form of subservience.

Subsequent tales by former deputies were also demeaning and served to tarnish Bass' name. The *Daily Oklahoma* of January 18, 1911, featured a story captioned: "LITTLE STORIES OF MEN WHOSE LIVES OVERFLOW WITH DANGER, Wildest Tales of Adventure and Excitement Never Equaled the Real Histories of United States Marshal Deputies Now Working in State of Oklahoma."

The article was written about the swearing-in of Chris Madsen, as Acting Marshal, and five other deputies. At the time current and former deputies gathered and recounted episodes of past years. Included in the group was Heck Thomas, who like Madsen, was the subject of books and articles though neither officer served longer in the Territory or more valiantly than Bass Reeves.

The article describes Thomas as, "[o]ne of the most fearless and successful deputy marshals in the Territory." However, as pointed out earlier in this writing, Heck Thomas failed to uphold the law and protect Black citizens in the face of a White mob.

The article noted that during the course of the exchange, Deputy Marshal Allen Goff spoke of Bass:

Makes me think of that old story of Bass Reeves, a Negro Deputy United States Marshal who was a celebrity in Indian Territory until he died at Muskogee two years ago. You recollect, Chris, when Bass killed his Negro cook hired all the good lawyers in Fort Smith to keep them from being on the other side, you know, when they tried him for it two years later. Well Bass was coming back into Fort Smith with a string of prisoners and a Negro cook that he allowed to carry a gun. Now Bass had a little dog that he was mighty fond of, carried him with him all the time, and he had taught the dog to beg for something to eat by standing up on his hind legs. The Negro cook got a grudge against Bass while they were still several days away from Fort Smith, and he took it out on the dog. Bass this was the way he told it, of course told the cook to quit several times, and this must have made him sullen. One night, when the prisoners were lying by the campfire chained together and Bass was back on his elbows with his Winchester by his side, that little dog stood up on his hind feet and danced up to the cook begging with his front paws, and the cook didn't do anything but empty a skillet of boiling grease down the dog's throat and grabbed for his pistol. Bass slipped his Winchester forward quicker and it went off right in the cook's face, and he pitched forward into the fire. Bass didn't pay any attention to him for a minute, since he knew he had winged him, but tried to help the little dog, which was dying a few feet away. Bass saw the dog die and then turned round to finish the nigger cook, but found his bullet had hit him right in the neck and shot his head so nearly off that when Bass kicked the body it rolled into the fire."

The Paris, Texas, News in 1941 ran a series of articles containing the recollections of Deputy Marshal Frank Dalton, who served in the Indian Territory during the 1880s. Entitled "Backward Glances," the article of August 6, 1941, read as follows:

FRANK DALTON AS U. S. OFFICER

*Tells of Days in Indian Territory
When Bootleggers Were Many*

Concluding his story of his life while a United States Deputy Marshal for the Federal Court in Fort Smith, Arkansas, in the early eighties, Frank Dalton said:

Not long after that (the killing of McGew who was wanted as a murderer), I started to Fort Smith with a bunch of prisoners. I had 16 of them and our mode of travel was to handcuff and shackle them and load them into a covered wagon with a driver for the team, who was unarmed, while my posse and I (there were two posse-men on this trip) were armed with Winchester saddle guns and two six-shooters apiece, and rode horseback.

Nothing of importance happened till we got to Holdenville where we met Marshal Crump. He was also bound for Fort Smith with a batch of prisoners from the Choctaw country and we traveled together until we reached the Poteau River, about two days march from Fort Smith, where we met Baz [sic] Reeves, a Negro Deputy Marshal, who worked in the Choctaw country. Baz had his nephew, Henry, a Negro about 18 years old, who did their cooking. He also had two bloodhounds that he used to trail prisoners who managed to escape.

We divided the night guard into two-hour shifts and Baz was to be next to the last one while I drew the last shift. He waked me at 4 o'clock and wrapped in his blanket and went to sleep after waking Henry to prepare breakfast. I woke a couple of my prisoners and one of Crump's to get breakfast for the prisoners, and then settled down on my blanket roll to smoke and wait for day light.

I had made the rounds of the prisoners a couple of times to see if everything was right and it was getting near time to wake everybody, when Henry, the cook, took a skillet of flour gravy off the fire and set it down to cool. A hound, I guess, thought it looked good and stuck her nose into it to investigate. It was still hot, and she let out a howl that could have been heard a mile. Baz, who was laying asleep, jumped up and pulling his six-shooter shot the Negro boy through the head, killing him instantly. I have always thought Baz did not know what he was doing, but being wakened out of a sound sleep fired at the first thing he saw. Be that as it may, I popped him over the head and we took him to Fort Smith with the other prisoners. He was tried for murder and sentenced to hang but because of his excellent record as an officer he was pardoned after spending about a year in Fort Smith Jail.

As the twin territories moved closer to statehood, contact between White, Black and Indian became more restrained and separated by color. The relationship between the races in schools and public places deteriorated as Whites sought to subordinate Black citizens by separation. Oppressive racial policies soon became established law. Although George Steele, as first territorial Governor, favored equality and integration, the first territorial legislature passed a separate school law. Thus, the way was paved for future segregation laws.

During the Parker years, Bass had been greeted with respect by Indians and those Whites legally settled in the Territory. Bass and the other deputies were often invited into their homes for dinner or for an overnight stay. Nothing was too good for those who "rode for Parker." In turn he felt that if they could all work together to assure a safe place, then the land would be what they would all make it.

Sadly, after the Parker years, sentiments changed. Hardly anyone spoke to Bass as he rode through towns and settlements with his prisoners. Instead, Bass was treated as if he were no different from the criminals he was transporting. While there was no way to reconcile the risking of his life for an ungrateful, indifferent citizenry, Bass had no choice. He simply continued to perform his sworn duty to the best of his ability.

Over the years, Bass made many enemies and there were numerous threats and assassination attempts against his life. The *Muskogee Times* Democrat reported an attempt made on his life as late as November 12, 1906, when he was riding home from serving papers in the Wybark community near Muskogee. He was shot at after dark while crossing under a railroad trestle. The would-be assassin's bullet sent showers of splinters over his head. Despite a published report, the family maintains he was never wounded; but in a shoot-out mentioned earlier, his belt was shot in two, a button was shot from his coat, and the bridle reins in his hands were cut by a bullet. To some superstitious family members, this was further evidence that he has led a "charmed life."

CHAPTER **SIXTEEN**
Betrayal and Burial of Bass Reeves

In 1896, the United States Supreme Court issued its infamous *Plessy v. Ferguson* decision, allowing states to legally adopt legislation which imposed a rule of separate but equal to justify racial segregation. Obviously, the doctrine of separate but equal really meant separate and unequal with Blacks receiving the lesser portion. For example, in the Oklahoma Territory, four territorial governors willfully violated the law establishing the National Guard and providing that one of such companies so formed shall be taken from among the colored residents of the Territory of Oklahoma. (Oklahoma Statutes 1903, 836)

The railroads also failed to provide equal accommodations for Black passengers. In many instances, even laws providing for separate yet equal application were not enforced, and separate and unequal became common policy.

Bass joined others who fought in vain against such segregation laws and strongly supported all efforts seeking their repeal. Despite rebuffs, Bass was confident of full and equal citizenship for Blacks after statehood was assured by the Oklahoma Enabling Act passed by Congress in 1906. The Act formally melded the two Territories into a single state and stipulated that the new state should provide the ballot "[to all citizens without regard to color or previous condition of servitude." The Act pointedly forbade the new constitution from infringing upon the political or civil rights of any person because of color or race.

In his inaugural speech, William Murray, President of the Constitutional Convention, signaled what sort of laws could be expected from the convention under the new government. He stated bluntly:

> *We should adopt a provision prohibiting the mixed marriages of Negroes with other races in this State, and provide for separate schools and give the Legislature power to separate them in waiting rooms and on passenger coaches, and all other institutions in the State. We have no desire to do the Negro an injustice. We shall protect him in his real rights ... and accept him as God gave him to us and use him for the good of society ... I appreciate the old darky—who comes to me talking softly in that humble spirit which should characterize their action and dealings with the white man, and when they thus come they can get any favors from me.**

---

*Proceedings of the Proposed State of Oklahoma held at Guthrie, Oklahoma, November 20, 1906, to November 16, 1907.

The credentials committee quickly voted to deny the seating of Black delegates, prompting the Guthrie Leader to conclude, "The Negro question is settled, Oklahoma is now the White man's country" (Guthrie Leader, November 28, 1907) The drafting of a provision for segregation in the state constitution was a top priority on the convention's agenda. Aware of these developments, President Theodore Roosevelt declared: "I want Oklahoma admitted during my administration, but if they keep the Jim Crow law in the Constitution, under the enabling act, I can't issue the statehood proclamation."[1]

In October 1907, a delegation of prominent Black citizens met with the President to protest Oklahoma's admission as a state. This was a final attempt to secure full and equal rights as citizens and to prevent discriminatory legislation in violation of the Enabling Act. Reportedly, Roosevelt was courteous but did not want to hear their complaints about the statehood issue. Contrary to his prior statement, he broke in by saying, "Please do not ask me not to sign it." (Shawnee Daily Herald, October 29, 1907) Roosevelt's proclamation in November 1907 made the State Constitution the governing law in the new State of Oklahoma. Contrary to the letter and spirit of the Enabling Act, segregation laws became the first order of business. The Constitution, at 50,000-plus words, the longest in any state, allowed separate schools for children of African descent and prohibited interracial marriages. Senate Bill No. 1 segregated citizens on railroad cars and in waiting rooms. Conductors aboard trains were empowered to eject passengers who violated the law and were not held liable for their actions in courts. Furthermore, the law provided no penalty for those railroads which did not provide equal facilities.

From the time Bass joined the Parker court in 1875 until statehood, he had dedicated his life to making the land a more fit and proper living place by protecting rights and promoting justice under the law. However, the opening of land primarily for

White settlement brought gross injustices in spite of the law. Early in his career, Bass could not have imagined that the unequal application of the law would become a widespread plague on America's legal system. Mob violence and lawlessness were followed by legally sanctioned measures against Black citizens denying them basic Constitutional rights and perverting the cause of justice. These developments were not only a betrayal of Bass Reeves, a lover and true defender of the law, but also of other like-minded Americans.

Bass welcomed an Oklahoma State Constitutional provision that the state could not deny any citizen the right to vote. Specifically, the Constitution declared: The State shall never enact any laws restricting or abridging the right of suffrage on account of race, color, or previous condition of servitude. For Bass, voting was the civil right to be cherished the most because it provided the means for citizens to determine the laws by which they would be governed and by whom they would be enforced. The lawman believed that the right to vote was the only hope to ensure that a government under laws would be a government under just laws.

The coming of statehood meant that the role of Deputy U. S. Marshal as a federal law enforcement officer would be assumed by newly-created state agencies. Furthermore, Bass was getting old and needing a rest. Although still active and appearing younger than his years, the strain of 32 years as a deputy was beginning to show. He had spent too many nights sleeping on the ground in the wet and cold. In addition, the countless days and nights spent in the saddle on manhunts further contributed to his deteriorating condition.

Like Judge Parker, law enforcement had become Bass' life. Because he had spent so many years as a lawman, he wanted to continue and accepted a position as a municipal police officer in Muskogee. Bass was pleased to be active and enjoyed the respect of the people he met. The Western Age of Langston made the following announcement.

> *NEGRO DEPUTY U.S. MARSHAL: A POLICEMAN*
>
> *Muskogee, Okla., Jan 2 - Former Deputy United States Marshal Bass Reeves, a giant Negro who was in many battles with outlaws in the wild days of Indian Territory and during Judge Parker's reign at Fort Smith is on the Muskogee police force. . . .*
>
> *He is now over 70 years old and walks with a cane ... He is as quick of trigger, however, as in the days when gunmen were in demand.*

After serving for almost two years, Bass' health deteriorated to the point that he had to permanently retire. It was said that during his period of service, there was not even a minor crime committed on his beat. On November 19, 1909, the Muskogee *Times Democrat* reported:

> *Bass Reeves, a deputy United States marshal in old Indian Territory for over thirty years, is very ill at his home in the fourth ward and is not expected to live.*
>
> *Reeves was a deputy under Leo Bennett in the last years of the federal regime in Oklahoma, and also served in the old days of Judge Parker at Fort Smith.*
>
> *In the early days when the Indian country was overridden with outlaws, Reeves was sent to go through*

the Indian country and gather up criminals which were tried at Fort Smith. These trips lasted sometimes for months and Reeves would herd into Fort Smith, often single handed, bands of men charged with crimes from bootlegging to murder. He was paid fees in those days which sometimes amounted to thousands of dollars for a single trip.

The veteran Negro deputy never quailed in facing any man. Chief Ledbetter says of the old man that he was one of the bravest men this country has ever known.

He was honest and fearless.

His son shot and killed his own wife and Reeves, enforcing the law, arrested his own son. The young Negro was sent to the penitentiary.

While the old man is slowly sinking, Bud, who for years was in the government service with Reeves, is a daily visitor at the Reeves home. Police Judge Walrond, who was United States district attorney while Reeves was an officer, also called on the old Negro.

While Reeves could neither read or write, said Judge Walrond today, he had a faculty of telling what warrants to serve any one and never made a mistake. Reeves carried a batch of warrants in his pocket and when his superior officer asked him to produce it the old man would run through them and never fail to pick up the one desired.

Bud Ledbetter had remained a friend of Bass for many years. In fact Bud Ledbetter was Chief of Police for the city of Muskogee, who hired Bass as a police officer in Muskogee. They had remained good friends over the years. Art Burton reported a story of Bass and his lawman days with Ledbetter:

Deputy Bud Ledbetter was in pursuit of a White outlaw near Gibson Station. I. T. Ledbetter and his posse were able to pin down the outlaw early in the day with gunfire. As the day progressed, Ledbetter and his posse did not make any gain in subduing the outlaw and by late afternoon had expended a large amount of ammunition. Ledbetter became very frustrated and requested the assistance of Bass Reeves. Reeves was brought to the scene of the shoot-out. At this time, the posse was still shooting at the outlaw; one of the deputies in the posse was W. B. Depue. The desperado decided to make a run for it on foot as daylight was fading. Posse members fired at the running target but missed. Ledbetter hollered, "Get 'em Bass." Bass replied, "I'll break his neck." At a distance of a quarter-mile, Bass, with one shot from his Winchester rifle, broke the outlaw's neck.[1]

Bass never recovered from the breakdown of his health. On January 12, 1910, he died at age 72 in Muskogee of Bright's disease. Bass was buried with great ceremony. In attendance were hundreds of old friends: Indian, White and Negro.

An obituary notice lauded Reeves' role in history:

...in the history of the early days of Oklahoma the name of Bass Reeves has a place in the front rank among those who cleaned out the old Indian

> *Territory of outlaws and desperadoes. No story of the conflict of the government's officers with those outlaws which ended only a few years ago with the rapid filling up of the territory with people, can be complete without mention of the old Negro who died yesterday.*
>
> *For thirty-two years, beginning way back in the seventies and ending in 1907, Bass Reeves was a deputy United States marshal. During that time he was sent to arrest some of the most desperate characters that ever infested Indian Territory and endangered life and peace in its borders. At times he was unable to get them alive ... but Bass Reeves always said he had never shot a man when it was not necessary for him to do so in the discharge of his duty to save his own life. (Muskogee Phoenix January 13, 1910)*

An article in the same newspaper on January 15, 1910, stated:

> *Bass Reeves, Negro, was buried yesterday and his funeral was attended by a large number of white people. Men who in the early days knew the old deputy marshal and admired him as a faithful officer and respected him as an honest man.*
>
> *Bass Reeves was a unique character. Absolutely fearless and knowing no master but duty, the placing of a writ in his hands for service meant that the letter of the law would be fulfilled though his life paid the penalty. In the carrying out of his orders during his thirty-two years as deputy United*

States marshal in the old Indian Territory days, Bass Reeves faced death a hundred times. The arrest of his own son for wife-murder, for which crime the young man is now serving a life sentence, is the best illustration of the old deputy's Spartan character. He performed that duty as he did all others entrusted to him and he was invariably given the worst cases with an eye single to doing his duty under the law.

Bass Reeves is dead. He was buried with high honors, and his name will be recorded in the archives of the court as a faithful servant of the law and a brave officer. And it was fitting that such recognition was bestowed upon this man. It is fitting that, black or white, our people have the manhood to recognize character and faithfulness to duty. And it is lamentable that we as white people must go to this poor, simple old Negro to learn a lesson in courage, honesty and faithfulness to official duty.

Within six months of Bass' death and in direct violation of the Oklahoma and United States Constitutions, the Oklahoma Constitution was amended to deny Black citizens the right to vote. At the same time, America welcomed immigrants to its shores and the Statue of Liberty was hailed as a prominent symbol of American democracy, representing the spirit of liberty and equality for all.

From his birth to his death, the law was a dominant force in Bass' life and attests to the truth of the scripture "that the law is good, if a man use it lawfully". Slavery, itself a creature of the law, was founded on the right of one human being to own another. Born into slavery, Bass actually violated the law when he escaped, because he was legally the property of another. However, when the Constitution was amended following the Civil War, Bass believed that a whole New World had been created. Slavery was abolished, and the concept of equality was elevated to the Constitutional level. In that atmosphere and influenced by the fervent devotion of Judge Parker to the Constitution and the law, he decided to dedicate his life to serving justice under law.

Tragically, after so many years of unswerving dedication to the rule of law, the cruel and unjust laws that had condemned Bass to slavery returned to haunt him in his final days. Considering all that had happened to him, it would seem that he would be filled with despair and view his life's work as having been in vain. But, even amidst apparent defeat, Bass never lost faith in America and the rule of law.

Back when Bass was a slave boy, Reba, the elderly slave woman, had told his mother, *"He's gon' see greatness, and he gon' see danger ... Others gon' make him a leader ..."* To a limited degree, Reba's prophecy was fulfilled. But in serving his country as an officer of the law, no American has more courageously demonstrated a commitment to our nation's ideals than United States Deputy Marshal Bass Reeves. Faith in God, love of family and pride in serving his country were the lights that guided his life.

CHAPTER **SEVENTEEN**
Newspaper Articles

As a Black lawman at this time in our history, Bass Reeves carried an immense burden. Although his actions were closely scrutinized, he was never deterred from the serious performance of his duties. In a discussion of the make-up of the U. S. Court at Fort Smith, it is noted that he was named one of the lead deputies.

> *This court is without doubt the largest criminal court in the United States. It is a district court with circuit court powers. Its jurisdiction extends over sixteen counties In Western Arkansas and the five civilized tribes of Indians .... The Deputy U.S.*

Marshals for Creek and Cherokee Nations are Andrew Smith, Elias Andrews, W. F. Jones, Bud T. Kell and Sam Sixkiller; for Choctaw Nation, Tyner Hughes, John Farr, Sam Wingo and J. W. Searle; for Chickasaw Naton, J. H. Mershon and John Williams; Seminole, Creek and Chickasaw Nations, Bass Reeves. There are many local deputies scattered throughout the district ...

Muskogee Indian Journal, October 22, 1885

Considering Bass' long record of service, newspaper accounts of his many arrests are uncommonly sparse. The following articles appeared in the *Fort Smith Elevator*, naming Bass and his prisoners.

August 11, 1882
Deputy Marshal Bass Reeves came in on Monday with sixteen prisoners, as follows:

W. S. Smith, violating revenue law-on bond; Austin Laflore, Jake Gardener, Charles Holmes, larceny; Dick Randolph, Thos. McGiesey, G. W. Brashears, Russell Rowland, introducing liquor in the Territory; Chas. McNally, Boss Kemp, Chas. Carter, N. R. Rozell, W. H. Wynne, assault with intent to kill; W. F Skeggs, Richard Robinson, arson.

October 27, 1882
The following deputies have reported since our last: Bass Reeves, with twelve prisoners, as follows: Julius Henshaw, Henry DeCourtney, J. A. Fowler, R. Lindsey, Paul Mosey, Cather Lamey, James Kinder, all whisky cases; Henry Hope, John and Albert Lynch, murder; W. T. Kline and Isaac Frazier, larceny.

January 5, 1883
Deputy Bass Reeves came in the day before Christmas with the following prisoners: J. M. Marshal, General Cooper, Jas. Rabbit, Thomas West, Dave Greenstock (Indians), Reed Wolford, Perry Chase (white), all charged with introducing and selling whiskey in the Territory.

August 20, 1883
Deputy Marshal Bass Reeves reported on Monday with the following prisoners, thirteen in all: Jeremiah Wilson, (white), Tommy Lowe, Cheeky, Jakey-meeko, Paddy (Indians), Caesar James, Isaac Frazier (negroes), all charged with larceny; Simon, Little George, Walleska, Scotsie Homalney, Wilsey Willow (Indians), all whisky cases; Phillip Jackson (negro), assault with intent to kill.

July 20, 1883
W.T. Haynes, a white man, was lodged in jail Wednesday by deputy Bass Reeves. He was caught as he was crossing the river with some two gallons of alcohol and whisky in his saddle bags, which he had just purchased in this city.

June 29, 1883
Deputy Bass Reeves reported same day with Compeachy, Buck and Charles Beavers, Edward Ellis, Jimmy Laney, Sampeechie, alias Samson, all Indians, charged with introducing; Toney Dailey and Dosell Coody, negroes, assault with intent to kill; Spony Harjo, Indian, murder. Compeechia, Coody and Dailey gave bond.

August 31, 1883
Another Load Just In
Since the above was in type Deputy Bass Reeves and posse W. McCauley, came in with ten more prisoners, as follows: Jonas

Thompson, Allen Taylor, Philip King, Dan Davis, James Kinder, Bamulchey, all Indians, charged with introducing; Leeharmony, Indian, Scott Wright, Aaron Wright, Silas Johnson, negroes, larceny.

December 7, 1883
Bass Reeves registered J. C. Hobaugh, M. B. Donaghey, J. P. McCaslin, white; Perry Bruner, colored; Pefarthusly and Tommy, Indians; all charged with larceny. Jordan Miles, colored, murder; Simmons, Ben Brown, alias Love; Little John, Joe Red mouth, Simon Bush, Ne-a-ho-la, Paulmuskey, Indians; Silvester Williams, colored; all charged with introducing; Emarthulchey, Indian, assault to kill.

February 8, 1884
Deputy Marshal Bass Reeves came in on Friday last with 12 prisoners: John Black (white) charged with murder; Joseph Sadler (white), assault with intent to kill; Wm. Hulsey, (Indian) larceny; J. B. Tumbull (white) Thomson Mitchee, Seybom, Sonny Harjo, alias Peters, Fleachy, Artisonubby, Parcheny, Geo. Bearhead, one Jessy (Indians) introducing whiskey in the Territory.

February 29, 1884
Horse Thief Jailed
On Monday last Robert Landers and Bill Wilson were arrested in this city by Deputy Marshals Wilson and Reeves, assisted by Charlie Laflore, of the Indian police. Landers has been here about three weeks, and was recognized by Laflore as a man who had stolen some horses at Gainesville, Texas, about six weeks ago, and for whom the Texas Stock Association offers a large reward. Laflore says he is one of a gang of thieves and robbers who have committed depredations in the Indian Territory, Texas and Missouri for some time. He recently robbed a man near

Cherokee Town of $120, and is said to be one of the gang who robbed the telegraph operation at Colbert Station a short time since. One of his pals was arrested a few days ago in the Nation and told of some of the plans of the gang, one of which was to rob Alex. McKinney, who lives between Stringtown and Atoka. Landers will likely be taken to Gainesville, the authorities there having been telegraphed to. He sold a horse at Van Buren a few weeks ago.

Wilson was released, there being no charges against him, his arrest growing out of the fact that he was the companion of Landers.

April 25, 1884

Deputies Reeves and Wilson came in Wednesday with the following prisoners: James Greeson, assault with intent to kill; Eleck Bruner, Aaron Sancho and Hotabisy, larceny; Crolsey Fixico, Tobey Hill, Golmo Jessee, Wiley Hawkins, Noah, Charley Jones, Amos Hill and G. H. Brewer, introducing spirituous liquors. One of their prisoners who was severely wounded while resisting arrest had to be left in the Territory, a physician saying that to move him would endanger his life.

May 29, 1885

A deputy's arrival with his prison wagon was a public event and, of course newsworthy: Deputy Bass Reeves came in Sunday from an extended trip through the Territory, bringing seventeen prisoners, who were registered at the jail's office as follows: Jonas Stake, Two-a-nuck-ey, one Wiley (Indians) charged with murder; Chas. Cosy, one Feglin, arson; Ben Bowlegs alias Ben Billy alias Williams (Indian), John Pickett, larceny; Robert Ken-a-wah, Joseph Dorsey, one Hawkins, Robert Kelly, Wolf alias Ya-gha, Barney alias Hills Harjo, one Winnie, one Siller, One Jennie (Indians), Adam Brady (Negro), introducing and selling whiskey in Territory. John Pickett gave bond.

July 31, 1885
Deputy Bass Reeves came in same evening with eleven prisoners as follows: Thomas Post, one Walaska, and Wm. Gibson, assault with intent to kill; Arthur Copiah, Abe Lincoln, Miss Adeline Grayson and Sally Copiah, alias Long Sally, introducing whiskey in Indian country; Jo E. Adams, Jake Island, Andy Alton and one Smith, larceny. Island, Alton, Lincoln and Smith gave bond. The others went to jail.

October 30, 1885
U. S. Marshal, Bass Reeves, came in on Monday evening last with 17 prisoners, among them were Hens Posey and one Deldrick, charged with murder. The others were John Robinson, assault with intent to kill; Robert Johnson, Wiley Kelly, Colbert Lasley and old man Cintop, larceny. The balance are all whiskey cases.

July 4, 1890
Deputy Bass Reeves came in Friday with Williams Roberts, charged with murder; William Trammell, William Cully, Robert Albert, Thomas Jefferson, Wilson Knight and Thomas Knight, all charged with introducing and selling liquor in Indian country. Cully and Jefferson gave bond.

May 28, 1891 (The Muskogee Phoenix)
Sunday night, about 12:30, officers Bass Reeves and Wiley McIntosh arrested W. H. McDonald and one Cords, charged with killing John Irvins, the man found murdered in Blue Creek, twelve miles west of Wagoner some two weeks ago. The officers had spotted the men some time ago and arrested them at their house near Blue Creek. The evidence against the two men is very strong. They were known to have threatened the life of Irvins and cannot well

account for themselves at the time the crime was committed. Our readers are familiar with the particulars of the finding of Irvin's body in the creek with a bullet hole in his head. The men were taken to Fort Smith and jailed.

Some accounts of Bass' more unusual adventures are noted:

March 27, 1885
Deputy U. S. Marshal Bass Reeves found a Negro man in jail at Gainesville, Texas, last week that he was sure was John Williams, the murderer of Constable Houck, of Van Buren. The Texas authorities turned him over to Bass, who brought him to Van Buren by rail, but he proved to be the wrong man. A Gainesville correspondent of the Fort Worth Gazette says Bass paid $100 reward to the Texas officers to get possession of the man. If that's the case, Bass is the loser.

One account attested to his phenomenal memory:

Deputy United States Marshal John Cordell arrived in Muskogee Monday with two prisoners, Barney Fixico, and an Indian named "Wild Cat," who was charged with the murder of Billy Culley, a prominent Seminole on February 3. Deputy Marshal Bass Reeves immediately identified "Wild Cat" as a prisoner who had escaped from him twenty years ago while the two were on their way to Fort Smith. It was supposed that "Wild Cat" was long since dead.

Some of the fugitives Bass sought were not prone to violence, but were guilty of "white collar" crimes:

December 26, 1884
E. D. Jones was arrested in Franklin County on Wednesday of last week as a fugitive from justice by Deputy Marshal Reeves. He was lodged in the U. S. jail on the following night, and on

Friday Chief Deputy C. M. Barnes left with him for Louisville, Ky., where there is an indictment against him for altering a mail contract. He was formerly a Kentucky mail contractor. He has a family in the Blue Grass State. He sent his wife $10 the morning he left.

Other examples of criminal conduct and attempts to escape have been reported:

Deputy Bass Reeves came in Sunday with Ed Walker. Walker is a colored gentleman who sometimes preaches, or as he puts it, he is an exhauster of the scriptures. His time and mind is not wholly given to the sacred book and its teachings, however, for occasionally he finds time to make love to the fair sex of his own color with satisfactory results to himself. In one particular, Walker is a Mormon, at least he believes in that doctrine to the extent that a man is entitled to as many wives as he can get, and for having more than one darling to love, obey and worship him, he was lodged in the U. S. jail to await the action of the court.

December 11, 1903 *(Chandler Tribune)*
BUTTED AWAY FROM OFFICER MUSKOGEE:
By using his head as a battering ram James Pryor, Negro, from Wybark, escaped arrest at the hands of Paul Smith, a posse-man under Deputy Marshal Bass Reeves, and is still at large.

Reeves and Smith were searching for Pryor, but had separated in order to find out if the man they sought was in a clump of bushes. As Smith stepped into the road he saw Pryor and advanced toward him. The Negro was armed with a Winchester rifle, but did not attempt to fire until close to Smith and his aim then was rendered inaccurate by Smith knocking down the muzzle of the gun. The two scuffled for a time, and while so doing Pryor managed to strike Smith a terrific blow on the head with his forehead. The white man fell to the ground unconscious and remained so for fully a half hour.

PICTORIAL PORTFOLIO

Ned Christie (Dead). Photo courtesy of Fort Smith National Historic Site.

Bass Reeves

THE BLACK BADGE

Bass Reeves (front row with cane) Muskogee, Indian Territory. White and Black policemen. c1900. Photo courtesy of Western History Collections, University of Oklahoma Library.

Bass Reeves (second row-left), pictured with Federal Official Family (including U.S. Marshals, U.S. Commission, U.S. District Attorney) November 16, 1907. Muskogee, Oklahoma. Photo courtesy of Fort Smith National Historic Site.

THE BLACK BADGE

Paul Brady's parental roots. Five generations (left to right) great-grandmother (Paralee), grandmother (Jane), Aunt Nettie, Cousin Ethel and her son, Lee Curtis. 1904.

Alice Spahn (Bass Reeves' daughter).

THE BLACK BADGE

Belle Starr (Famous Lady Outlaw). Photo courtesy of Oklahoma Historical Society.

Cherokee Bill (Cherokee Outlaw) and his mother, Mrs. Ellen Lynch. Photo courtesy of Western History, Universtiy of Oklahoma.

Ned Christie (Cherokee Outlaw). Photo courtesy of Fort Smith National Historic Site.

Isaac C. "Hanging Judge" Parker. Photo courtesy of Fort Smith National Historic Site.

THE BLACK BADGE

Judge Brady and Bass Reeves Monument dedicated to Muskogee, and positioned at Muskogee, Oklahoma City Hall.

Judge Parker holds court in his court room in Ft. Smith, Arkansas. Photo courtesy of Fort Smith National Historic Site.

Bass Reeves' arrest warrant for Fayette Barnett and Belle Starr.

58

UNITED STATES
vs
Larceny

Fayette Barnett
&
Belle Starr

Information filed and Capias and Subpœna
issued Sept 11 1885
STEPHEN WHEELER,
U. S. Commissioner

OCT 30 1885

United States of America,
Western District of Arkansas.

The President of the United States,

TO THE MARSHAL OF THE WESTERN DISTRICT OF ARKANSAS—GREETING:

WHEREAS, Complaint on oath hath been made before me, charging that *Fayette Barnett Belle Starr* .... did, on or about the 15 day of May A. D. 1885, in the Indian Country, Western District of Arkansas .... Commit Larceny .... contrary to the form of the statute in such cases made and provided, and against the peace and dignity of the United States.

Now, therefore, you are hereby commanded, in the name of the President of the United States of America, to apprehend the said *Fayette Barnett Belle Starr* .... and bring their .... bodies forthwith before me, STEPHEN WHEELER, Commissioner appointed by the United States District Court for said District, whenever they may be found that they .... may be then and there dealt with according to law for said offense.

GIVEN under my hand this 11 day of August ...., 1885, in the one hundred and tenth year of our Independence.

Stephen Wheeler Commissioner U. S. Dist. Court, West. Dist. Ark.

SELECTED BIBLIOGRAPHY

Addington, Wendell G., *Slave Insurrections in Texas, Journal of Negro History, XXXV.* (October 1950): 408-434.

Black History in Oklahoma - a resource book. Edited by Kay M. Teall. Oklahoma City Public Schools, 1971.

Burton, Arthur T., *Black, Red and Deadly: Black and Indian Gunfighters of the Indian Territory,* 1870-1907. Austin: Eakin Press, 1991.

Burton, Jeffrey, *Indian Territory and the United States,1866-1906: Courts, Government, and the Movement forOklahoma Statehood.* Norman: University of Oklahoma Press, 1995.

Chapman, Berlin B., *Freedmen and the Oklahoma Lands, Southwestern Social Science Quarterly, XXIX* (September, 1948) 150-159.

Cherokee Advocate, 31 May 1902.

The Chickasaw Enterprise, 28 November 1901.

Croy, Homer, *He Hanged Them High: An Authentic of the Fanatical Judge Who Hanged Eighty-Eight Men.* New York: Duell, Sloan and Pearce, 1951. Boston: Little, Brown and Company, 1952.

Trigger Marshall: The Story of Chris Madsen. New York, Duell, Sloan and Pearce, 1958. *Daily Oklahoman,* 25 August 1901, 26 August 1904.

Durham, Phillip, and Jones, Everett L., *The Negro Cowboys.* New York: Dodd, Mead and Company, 1965.

The Federal Courts of the Tenth Circuit: A History. Edited by James K. Logan. Denver: U.S. Court of Appeals for the Tenth Circuit.

Foreman, Grant, *The Five Civilized Tribes.* Norman: University of Oklahoma Press, 1934. *Indian Removal: The Emigration of the Five Civilized Tribes of Indians.* Norman: University of Oklahoma Press, 1932.

Fort Smith Elevator 15 April 1887; 13 May 1887.

Franklin, Jimmie Lewis, *Journey Toward Hope: A History of Blacks in Oklahoma.* Norman: University of Oklahoma Press, 1982.

Gibson, Arrell M., *Oklahoma: A History of Five Centuries.* Norman: Harlowe Publishing Corporation, 1965.

Gideon, D.C., *Indian Territory, Descriptive, Biographical and Genealogical Including The Landed Estates, County Seats, Etc. with a General History of the Territory.* New York and Chicago: Lewis Publishing Company, 1901.

Gregg, Kale Leila. *The Road to Santa Fe: The Journal and Diaries of George Champlin Sibley and Others Pertaining to the Surveying and Marking of a Road from the Missouri Frontier to the Settlements of New Mexico, 1825-1827.* Albuquerque: University of New Mexico Press, 1952.

The Gunfighters: New York: Time-Life Books, 1974.

SELECTED BIBLIOGRAPHY

Harman, Samuel W., *Hell on the Border: He Hanged Eighty-Eight Men.* Fort Smith, Arkansas: Phoenix Publishing Company, 1898.

Harrington, Fred Harvey. *Hanging Judge.* Caldwell, Idaho: Caxton Printers, 1951.

Indian Chieftain, 24 September 1896; 29 August 1901.

Interviews, Indian Pioneer History. Indian Archives Division, Oklahoma Historical Society, Oklahoma City.

Katz, William Loren, *The Black West: A Documentary and Pictorial History.* New York: Doubleday and Company, Inc., 1971.

Littlefield, Daniel, and Underhill, Lonnie E., *Negro Marshals in the Indian Territory, The Journal of Negro History LVI* (April 1971).

Leckie, William H., *The Buffalo Soldiers: A Narrative of the Negro Cavalry in the West.* Norman: University of Oklahoma Press, 1967.

Marriott, Alice, and Rachlin, Carol K., *Oklahoma, The Forty-Sixth Star.* Garden City, New York: Doubleday and Company, Inc., 1973.

McReynolds, Edwin C., *A History of the Sooner State.* Norman, University of Oklahoma Press, 1954.

Mooney, Colonel Charles W., *Doctor in Belle Starr County.* Oklahoma City Century Press, 1954.

Muskogee Daily Phoenix, 24 March 1898; 13 January 1910.

Muskogee Times Democrat, 19 November 1909.

Oklahoma City Weekly Times Journal, 8 March 1907, 23 August 1907.

Prassel, Frank Richard. *The Western Peace Officer: A Legacy of Law and Order.* Norman: University of Oklahoma Press, 1972.

Shawnee Daily Herald, 29 October 1907.

Shirley, Glenn, *Law West of Fort Smith.* New York: Henry Holt and Company, 1957.

Heck Thomas, The Story of a Real Gunfighter. New York and Philadelphia: Chilton Company, 1962.

Belle Starr and Her Times: The Literature, the Facts, and the Legends. Norman: University of Oklahoma Press, 1982.

West of Hell's Fringe Crime: Criminals and the Federal Peace Officer in Oklahoma Territory, 1889-1907. Norman: University of Oklahoma Press, 1978.

Speer, Bonnie Stahlman, *The Killing of Ned Christie.* Norman: Reliance Press, 1990.

Stampp, Kenneth M., *The Peculiar Institution: Slavery in the Ante-Bellum South.* New York Vintage Books, 1956.

Tolson, Arthur Lincoln, *The Negro in Oklahoma Territory, 1889-1907: Study in Racial Discrimination.* Ph.D. diss., University of Oklahoma, 1966.

Williams, Nudie E., *United States vs. Bass Reeves:*

Selected Bibliography

Black Lawman on Trial, The Chronicles of Oklahoma LXVIII (Summer 1990).

REFERENCES

PREFACE

1. D.C. Gideon, *Indian Territory* (New York: Lewis Publishing Company, 1901) 115

PROLOGUE

1. The story with dialect was related by Ethel Burks, Paralee's great-granddaughter. In Paralee's later years, Ethel was her caregiver. Reba was a "conjurer," one who could cast spells unknown to Whites. Conjurers had a powerful influence over fellow slaves. Often powers were derived from a small bag of animal bones, powdered snake skins, horse hair ashes, and blood mixed with graveyard dirt.

CHAPTER I

1. Wendell G. Addington, *Slave Insurrections in Texas*. Journal of Negro History (October 1950), 431

2. Harold Schoen, *The Free Negroes and the Texas Revolution*, Southwestern Historical Quarterly XL (July, 1936), 26-34

CHAPTER II

1. Addington, 408

2. Ibid, 418

CHAPTER III

1. John Meserve, *Chief Opotheleyahola*, Chronicles of Oklahoma, Vol. IX (December, 1931), 441-442

2. Larry Rampp, *Negro Troop Activity in Indian Territory*, Chronicles of Oklahoma, Vol. 47 (Spring, 1964), 547

3. Congress had stipulated that the regiments were to have White commanders. While George A. Custer refused to command such a unit, John J. Pershing, later deemed a hero for his command during World War I, headed the Tenth Calvary. "It has been an honor," Pershing later declared, "which I am proud to claim to have been at one time a member of that intrepid organization of the Army which has always added glory to the military history of America, the 10th Calvary."

4. Alice Marriott and Carol K. Rachlin; *Oklahoma, the Forty-Sixth Star*, (Carden City, NY: Doubleday and Company, Inc. 1973), 49

CHAPTER IV

1. In September 1976, Mount Olive Methodist Church was added to the National Register of Historical Places. The church holds the distinction of being the oldest African-

REFERENCES

American Church west of the Mississippi River. Bass' great-niece, Mildred Landfair, participated in the re-dedication service celebrating its 107th year.

CHAPTER V

1. Glen Shirley, *Law West of Fort Smith* (Lincoln: University of Oklahoma Press, 1995), IX

CHAPTER VI

1. *Oklahoma Star*, November 30, 1875

CHAPTER VII

1. Criminal Jacket #120, Western District of Arkansas, Fort Smith, W151 Federal Records Depository Center, Fort Worth, Texas; (hereafter cited as FRDC)

2. *Fort Smith Elevator*, April 15, 1887; May 13, 1887

3. *Arkansas Gazette*, September 4, 1875; *St. Louis Republican*, September 4, 1875

CHAPTER VIII

1. Adam Grayson, Indian-Pioneer History (Indian Archives Division, Oklahoma Historical Society, Oklahoma City) LXXXIV (hereafter cited as Indian-Pioneer History), 336-339

2. *Fort Smith New Era*, June 1, 1881; Fort Smith Elevator, June 3, 1881

3. S. W. Harmon, *Hell on the Borders* (Fort Smith: Phoenix Publishing Company, 1898), 570

4. Charles Mooney, Doctor in *Belle Starr Country* (Oklahoma City: Century Press, 1975), 189

CHAPTER IX

1. Nancy Pruitt, *Indian-Pioneer History*, (History Archives Divi-sion, Oklahoma Historical Society, Oklahoma City) LXI 429

2. Criminal Jacket #216, Western District of Arkansas, Fort Smith, W151, FRDC

3. Criminal Jacket #120, FRDC

4. Criminal Jacket #85 FRDC; *Fort Smith Elevator*, Decenber 31, 1886

5. *Fort Smith Elevator*, August 18, 1882

6. Weekly *Times Journal* (Oklahoma City), March 8, 1907

CHAPTER X

1. Criminal Jacket #12 FRDC

2. Ibid

3. Criminal Jacket #160 FRDC

4. D. C. Gideen, *Indian Territories,* 115, 116

CHAPTER XI

1. Shirley, 146

2. Arell M. Gibson, Oklahoma: *A History of Five Centuries* (Norman: Harlow Publishing Corporation, 1965), 294-295

3. Berlin Chapman, Freedom and the Oklahoma Lands, Southwestern Social Science Quarterly, XXIX (September, 1948), 150

4. *The Missouri Republican*, January 27, 1888; April 23, 1888

5. Holocomb to S. J. Kirkwood, April 25, 1881, S. Ex. Docs. 47th Cong. 1 Sess., (1990)

6. Price to Sec. Int., July 5, 1882, S. Misc. Docs., IV (1996) quoted in Tolson, 6

7. Chapman, 157

8. Commissioner Atkins to Sec. Int., March 22, 1886, Office of Indian Affairs, *L. Letter Book*, National Archives, Vol. 146 III

9. Chapman, 155

10. Washington Bee, July 1889

11. Oklahoma Chietain, March 6, 1890

12. Norman Transcript, March 8, 1890

CHAPTERS XII

1. Mooney, Doctor Jesse, 117
2. Ibid, 115
3. Bonnie Speer, *The Killing of Ned Christie* (Norman: Reliance Press, 1990), 1
4. *Indian Chieftain,* November 27, 1890
5. *Muskogee Daily Phoenix,* January 29, 1891
6. Ibid, February 5, 1891
7. Speer, 11
8. Speer, 6
9. Shirley, 131
10. *Fort Smith Elevator,* March 20, 1896
11. Harmon, 431
12. Gideon, 18
13. Criminal Jacket #284 FRDC
14. Criminal Jacket #75 FRDC

CHAPTER XIII

1. *Fort Smith Elevator,* February 8, 1895
2. *St. Louis Republic,* September 18, 1896

3. Ibid

CHAPTER XIV

1. *Muskogee Phoenix,* January 13, 1910

CHAPTER XV

1. *San Francisco Examiner,* March 3, 1890

2. *Oklahoma City Times Journal,* August 23, 1907

3. *Alva Review,* April 10, 1902

4. Glenn Shirley, Heck Thomas: *Frontier Marshal* (Philadelphia: Chilton Company, 1962) 224

5. *Oklahoma Guide,* April 10, 1902

6. Ibid, June 23, 1902

7. *Indian Chieftain,* September 24, 1896

8. *Muskogee Phoenix,* March 24, 1898

9. *Oklahoma Guide,* July 26, 1904; Muskogee Cimeter, August 4, 1904

10. Ibid

CHAPTER XVI

1. Arthur T. Burton, *Black, Red and Deadly, Black and Indian Gunfighters of the Indian Territory* 1870-1907 (Austin: Eakin Press, 1991), 171

BOOK AVAILABLE THROUGH
Milligan Books, Inc.

The Black Badge $22.95

Order Form
Milligan Books, Inc.
1425 W. Manchester Ave., Suite C, Los Angeles, CA 90047
(323) 750-3592

Name_____ Date _____

Address _____

City_____ State____ Zip Code _____

Day Telephone _____

Evening Telephone _____

Book Title _____

Number of books ordered___ Total ....$ _____

Sales Taxes (CA Add 8.25%) ....$ _____

Shipping & Handling $4.90 for o`ne book .....$ _____

Add $1.00 for each additional book ....$ _____

Total Amount Due ....$ _____

☐ Check ☐ Money Order ☐ Other Cards _____

Visa   ☐ MasterCard Expiration Date _____

Credit Card No. _____

Driver License No._____

Make check payable to Milligan Books, Inc.

_____ _____
Signature   Date